D0401450

"Fasting for Ramadan is a remarkable book: an intensely personal meditation—shot through with poetry, philosophy, revelation, and doubt—on one of the world's great spiritual practices."

— Toby Lester, *Atlantic* contributing editor and author of *The Fourth Part of the World*

"Like a flower wilting in a dry pot, Ali's body grows weary without food and water. But as the days go on some other form of sustenance takes over to revive and replenish him, propelling him forward.... [An] incisive look at what it really means to be Muslim in today's world...."

— Samina Ali, novelist, author of *Madras on Rainy Days*

"This is an important book...written 'in that third voice, a voice between two people, neither one nor the other, neither embodied nor disembodied.' I have wanted to know what fasting in Islam involves, to admire its intentions and effects in solitude. Friends who have slipped away to pray, or who have cooked all day for the meal at night, without picking or tasting, are now more known to me. I am grateful for the time and attention that went into this book and I hope that multitudes will find their way to it, too."

— Fanny Howe, poet, novelist, and essayist, author of *The Winter Sun: Notes on a Vocation* and *Radical Love*

"[Kazim Ali] has quietly emerged as one of the indispensable voices of our aesthetic and geo-political moment. No writer now working...is more adept at articulating a mystical, beatific spirituality equally rooted in his Islamic faith and the concreteness of the secular world...."

— R. D. Pohl, The Gusto Blog, *Buffalo News*

Also by Kazim Ali

FASTING FOR RAMADAN

kazim ali

NOTES FROM A
SPIRITUAL PRACTICE

Tupelo Press
North Adams, Massachusetts

Library of Congress Cataloging-in-Publication Data
Ali, Kazim, 1971-
Fasting for Ramadan / Kazim Ali.
    p.   cm. -- (Tupelo Press lineage series)
ISBN: 978-1-932195-94-1 (pbk. : alk. paper)
1. Ramadan--Anecdotes. I. Title.
BP186.4.A455 2011
297.3'62--dc22

                                                        2010053815

Cover and text designed by Josef Beery.
Cover photo: iStockphoto. Used with permission.

First paperback edition: April 2011.

Tupelo Press
P.O. Box 1767, North Adams, Massachusetts 01247
Telephone: (413) 664-9611 / Fax: (413) 664-9711
editor@tupelopress.org / www.tupelopress.org

Tupelo Press is an award-winning independent literary press that publishes
fine fiction, non-fiction, and poetry in books that are a joy to hold as well as
read. Tupelo Press is a registered 501(c)3 non-profit organization, and we
rely on public support to carry out our mission of publishing extraordinary
work outside the realm of large commercial publishers. Financial donations
are welcome and are tax deductible.

 Supported in part by an award from
the National Endowment for the Arts

NATIONAL
ENDOWMENT
FOR THE ARTS

To Gul-baji,

my Flower Sister, my Silver Scholar—

Contents

Preface

The first part of this book originated as a blog that was posted daily. In this form of immediacy I tried to think about fasting, spiritual discipline, and my own ideas about these.

But several years earlier I had kept a little fasting journal in a spiral notebook, writing privately, just for myself.

If the first (and written later) portion of this book is read as the mind's reaching out, with the intention of external communication, then the second (and written earlier) portion could be understood as grounded in the body and the body's experience, which was internal, a practice of reflection.

Of course, always there is traffic between reflection and expression, as between the mind and the body, between god and human, between past and present, between the external system of the world and the internal system of the so-called self.

Why two books belong between the same

covers, why two books are really one book, and why the later book is first and the earlier second:

Because on Eid-ul-Fitr, the celebration at the end of the fasting month, when traveling to the mosque for special prayers you are supposed to take one route going and another, different route coming home.

KA

29 Ramadan 1431

New Moon in the Western Sky:
Ramadan Essays

First Thoughts on Ramadan

The month of fasting begins tomorrow, August 22, though this is not universally accepted, as it depends on the actually barest crescent of the moon being sighted.

Growing up, fasting was my favorite spiritual practice; it still is, though arduous. One feels, at the end of a day of fasting, like a tree branch or a bone bleached in the sun.

I learned to pronounce the name of "Ramadan" only after Islam and the practices of Muslims came more into mainstream public discourse. This pronunciation, an Arabic one, with three syllables and a hard "d," is not the way I had always spoken it before, in my Urdu-speaking home, where one would say, in only two syllables: "Ramzan." Sometimes even your own language disappears.

Did no one sense irony when Bill Clinton delayed, by three days, one of the bombing missions over Iraq because it would have fallen on Eid-ul-Fitr, the celebration concluding Ramzan? Instead the mission began on December 25. As if there weren't Iraqi Christians.

Today I am thinking of practical things: stocking up on high-nutrition foods, working out how I will do housework, exercise, and comment on student writing within the few hours of darkness I will have at the beginning and end of each day, because during the fast, the mind moves farther and farther away from temporality and detail-oriented work.

I love, at a difficult point in the fast—usually midafternoon—to engage a simple chore like sweeping a room or clearing a table.

Pattern of the fast: Wake in the predawn. Prepare your food and eat before the rise of the sun. During the day one must abstain from: all food and water. But also from: cigarettes, gossip or slander, sexual activity.

One cannot, during a fast, immerse one's head under water, breathe deeply of strong scents, needlessly tempt oneself with food, or otherwise attempt vicarious relief from the fast.

Pattern: In the first part of the day, one feels bold and energetic from the food just consumed. At a certain point you do not feel hungry so much as you feel the ebb of that energy. One is supposed to avoid exertion in order to better focus on the fast.

During the long mid-afternoon, one disappears into oneself. At some point I find myself retreating to my darkened bedroom, breeze blowing through, just to lie down and read or to take a nap.

At the end of the fast, you are almost not even hungry, but eat just because fast-breaking time has come and eating is what you have to do.

The cells of the body are constantly rejuvenating and replacing themselves. One cannot do something only once and feel the full benefits sink into the patterns of the body.

And so with the fast. Twenty-nine or thirty days of this.

Twenty-nine or thirty days to explore the line between the interior of the body and the surrounding world, to think about what is brought to us and what we owe.

And what if a human is not a separate entity after all but a microcosmic amalgamation of universal energy?

Tell me the difference between entity and eternity.

First Day

MORNING

I woke easily this morning, with anticipation. I had a crazy plan—since I couldn't run during the day, I would wake up early before *seheri* (morning meal) and run then; after the run I would come home, eat and drink in preparation for the fast.

For a moment, though the fire in my body wanted to burn, I remembered the long day of fasting ahead and realized: I had to find a new metaphor other than fire.

The point of the fast is not to flagellate yourself to nothing, but to sharpen your attention, to diminish your worldly attention and distractions so you can better perceive what is actually around you. I know at some point during the month physical activity will help me toward this goal, but I wanted a gentler start. I went for a walk instead.

Through the dark streets of Oberlin. Finally it is cool here. I will now confess to you I have a dangerous fear of the dark. I do not like basements. I turn on all the lights when no one is home. On the streets I am always looking for the murderer or the bandit.

This morning though, in the town I know, the only town I have lived in for longer than two years (not including Rhinebeck, dream of a home, where I lived from 2001 to 2004), I am starting to actually feel like I belong some place. To some place. That a place belongs to me.

To be abroad in the dark. To have not eaten. Looking at the buildings, the streets, thinking about what it is going to be like when I am teaching classes, walking with friends, socializing. "Is this place even real?" I wonder. The immediate corollary of which is: "Am I even real?"

After returning home I ate ice cream first. Home-made and dairy-free, from the recipe that one of my students sent me. Sweetness comes to me from every direction. Then I chopped a pear, made oatmeal, soaked the pear in the oatmeal, added soy milk, brown rice powder.

I drank two glasses of water but I think I drank them too fast. I have to sip over the course of an hour or two to make sure all the water goes in me.

Early in the morning, and I am empty. I am grateful for the emptiness. It occurred to me to practice some yoga *asana*, work on a little translating. I made no plans with anyone today, so I am in my house alone. My friend Chelsey is coming home from Portland. I asked her to call. I hope she calls.

As you turn from the outside to the inside it is nice to have some people around you to remind you that the other part of you is still there, has not gone in the night.

Because, after all, the fast is a practice that is meant to end. Which means even if you come to a realization about the illusions and temporality of the world, the fragility of the body, you are still supposed to come back to both.

AFTERNOON AND EVENING

The day is a hallway I am

walking through.

Every moment seems continuous and without pause.

Soundtrack: Alice Coltrane, *Translinear Light*.

My quick temper flattens.

Hours left but I am restless at home, unable to fix my mind on any task, so I walk into town.

It is cold for August, thank god.

Practicalities drift across my mind: steel wool, a new calendar, psyllium husks.

The days will get shorter.

I'm invited to go along to a social gathering but
I don't know if I can spend time among others
though I really want to go. How small and tender
the ego is.

Someone is downstairs in the kitchen cooking din-
ner for me.

It is nice to eat at the end of the day, but even nicer
to be taken care of.

Second Day

How easy to be drawn from attention to the world around me.

Not wanting to be irritable, I find it almost too much effort to talk to the people around me about quotidian things: who missed a meeting, who was supposed to sweep in the dining room, where the lost keys are.

But am I supposed to forget about these things and be a swirl of spiritual attention?

Marco is going to a canning workshop this morning. He said: You could come with me.

I said: I don't know how fasting is for other people, but for me—I don't even know who I am right now.

Who am I then, uncoupled from the basic foundational human desire: To feed oneself, the root of any desire. Am I still human? Or is a part of me reaching toward the arena that isn't?

And if that's the case, then the fact that the fast is a daily routine, ending each twilight, does seem like spiritual ADD. Reach for what's beyond, come back, reach for what's beyond, come back.

In yoga practice we learn to associate an inhale and an exhale with each movement through a *vinyasa*, but in held postures we also find the flow of breath—inhale, exhale, inhale, exhale. Inhale lengthen, exhale stretch deeper. There is a constant pulse to breath, as there is to the circulation of blood through the human body: rush out, rush back, rush out, rush back.

If our entire life is one side, our entire death another, if the entire daylight fast is one side, the entire night another, what if the shifting between spiritual attention and physical attention to the facts of the world, and the ability to maintain that balance, is the entire point?

Tempting to think so, but I think there is no "entire point" to fasting, the oddest of puzzles: that which has a hundred and one solutions.

Last night one of the cats knocked over a cup of water onto my books. I was so distraught I could have wept. A day of equipoise and blissing out in the fast did not so much evaporate from me as suddenly stand out in sharp relief to the parts of me that were still very tied to material existence.

Another benefit of the fast: You learn who you are and then who you really are. And who you really are is not always as close to or as far from who you are as you imagined. But you never really know, do you?

But I think one of the tricks I need to learn is how to manage both. As the month progresses, I will have to learn how to fast *and* how to sweep the dining room *and* find the lost keys.

3 *Third Day*

MORNING

What is one divided by zero? This is a mathematical equation I have always wanted to solve because I believe in the union of all created things, the bond we share beyond the purely molecular, which any scientist will confirm for you.

And I also believe in the cosmic version of *duende*: all the dark matter of the universe, the zero that no one can add up.

In the dark I came instantly awake.

So much energy in the morning. Last night I wilted, exactly like a flower without water. Remembering those slow-motion videos I had seen of flowers in a vase. Which show that over the course of three or five days cut flowers thrash.

This morning, third into the month, I ran. For about four miles. And in the run I felt, I really felt, my body: the way it moved, as a physical and kinetic thing, breath and blood moving through.

If you remember, I am afraid of the dark. Irrational, yes, but isn't most fear? Perceptions, the Yoga Sutras teach us, are based on past memories and experiences. One hopes, through a practice of yoga, to be able to perceive things as they are, not chained to all of our own messiness, the "fluctuations of our mind's consciousness."

So I was running along, listening to Girlyman sing to me through my headphones—particularly a wonderful song called "The Shape I Found You In," which I imagine to be a song between me and an old teacher of mine, Jonji Provenzano, who taught me from 2002 until he passed away last year.

I came to a dark place in the road, not illuminated by streetlights. I came to a part of the song that was about death. I thought: Here I go—at a place in my life, now or some point years from now, where I will never know—I will round a corner from life into death. Like that. Like this.

What was my first reaction: Fear. Close second: Wonder.

I saw in the road long streaks of black that seemed to me to be like Arabic writing. I thought: the Quran is here, even now, written on the road in front of me. Not to "reassure" me about death but to say: Even here, even now.

And I remembered one of my favorite verses: "Even if all the trees of the world were made into pens and all the oceans made into ink, with seven more oceans to multiply them, still the words of God would not come to an end". (Luqman, 27).

Even in the moments when I most doubted, I have loved this verse. Because it is precisely about doubt: If the words are eternal then the reading must be, too. God, the master of efficiency, hardly repeats himself. Even in the Quran, when a story is told a second time, it is told differently.

My grandfather, Sajjad Sayeed, was fond of saying, on the question of religion, "All rivers flow into the same ocean." Not until years later did I find this saying in the writings of the *Vedanta* scholar Swami Vivekananda. And years after that, I found it again in the writings of the Sufi poet Hafiz.

What I believe in, at least, is multiplicity; beyond multiplicity—though I am as yet unready to understand its true implications—I believe in infinity.

4 *Fourth Day*

MORNING

When fasting flattens out my desires, the manic motions of my mind, the sharp edges, I think: Maybe I could fill a bowl of this and carry it into the night, carry it into the part of my life when I am eating, functioning again.

So far I am trying and failing. Each night soon after I've eaten—the glorious gratitude for food again!—I've gotten upset about something, or irritated. I'm either saving up all the fire that has been on slow burn throughout the day, or the body, accustomed now to functioning without the energy of food, is completely disoriented by the influx of sugar, calories, other energies.

The body and the mind: Which is responsible for the moods of the self? Likely both. And my yoga study reminds me that the "moods" of the self are not the self, the self that abides.

I think there is a self that abides. A version of me skulking inside, watching everything that happens. Like in classical Indian music: there is a plucked melody but also a drone in the background, a constant note.

It's not one or the other that makes the music but the two, the thing that changes and the thing that doesn't.

So the fast doesn't bring you to your true self; no, fasting just tries to shine a light a little bit on the part that doesn't change, the constant part, the part you don't always see because you are governed by the passions of the physical and the temporal—of course that is the part of the body that depends on food—to stay alive, to function.

Each day is another chance to try.

This morning I woke to a rich Spanish tortilla (not like a little chip, but a thick omelet made with potatoes, onions, spices and other forms of goodness) made by one of my housemates. As I ate with gratitude I thought about the three other people I live with, realizing that I haven't really sat down with them to try to talk about the fast, what fasting means to me, what happens to me as I undertake it.

Fasting, like so many Islamic practices, is a community practice. But I don't have much community here. I have invited the Muslim Student Association members to come to *iftar*—evening fast-breaking— each Friday of the month. But mostly, on a day-to-day basis, I am on my own in the practice. My friend

Craig tells me the word for "one" in Arabic is *wahid*, the word for loneliness, *waheed*.

When I was growing up, once I was able, my mother and I always fasted the full month together. Fasting was something we shared, a secret we held between us. Waking early in the predawn, eating food, washing the dishes together.

Then throughout the day you knew there was someone else in the house who was in the same condition as you were.

And at the end of the fast, at the beginning of darkness, we would prepare food and eat together. I would watch her as she ate her first mouthful.

In all the distance since then—all the time that has passed, all the miles between us—when I remember those moments, I only feel intimacy, the immediacy of that sharing.

It is odd for me, because I have always been a loner. Always been lonely. I'm not much for the group practice and don't often go to community prayers.

Yet in my daily life: I'm garrulous, a talker. You would never know how alarmingly secretive I am, how much I don't want people to know what I am really thinking. How almost ashamed I am.

But when I fast I always reach out around me. I want everyone to know what is happening.

I feel there is something in my hands that I have to spill.

And by fasting, perhaps, I am not emptying the bowl of myself, but filling it, filling it, filling it.

Food, and attention to food, disappears—so what rushes into that space?

Filling myself, yes, but with what?

 *Fifth Day*

This morning the routine began to feel normal: to wake in darkness, to lace up my sneakers, hit the road, all in darkness. I waved to a worker who drives a water truck up and down the streets of Oberlin watering the bowls of flowers that hang from every street light. I see him each morning, around the same time, watering.

Last night as I broke my fast I was not ravenous. I ate some almonds, some berries, drank some water, and then didn't eat a full meal until about an hour later.

Is it starting to feel ordinary? If so, there will be time enough for fasting to become arduous again—I'm not even done with the first week.

But I can use this moment to move into greater attention. During the first few days of the fast, the fact that I was "not eating" became the central focus, an active practice of restraint. That feeling is falling away a little now. In yoga, there are eight stages (not really linear but simultaneous); the first of these is *yama*, or restraint. Following this is *niyama*, or active practices.

We will see where the fast leads me.

I noticed on the first day that when I wrote in the afternoon, in the height of foodlessness, my language splintered into short little sentences. Since then I've wanted to write in the afternoon and evening but haven't found my way.

This is not the first time I have written a Ramadan journal. The first time was in 2007, and those entries I wrote mostly in the afternoons and evenings. I considered including some of those entries here but decided I wanted this to be immediate writing, grounded in present experience.

Fasting teaches you this: You have to move slowly; you have this moment, and this moment alone holds the entire universe.

The body is a planet after all—all its strange parts, the wisdom tooth, the cerebellum, the epithelial tissue, the clavicle. Every single part functions together.

I knew in my bones—literally, I suppose—that there were no "vesitigial organs." Only very recently have scientists discovered purposes for both the spleen and the appendix. There are aspects of the world we are not even close to understanding. "So man has gone to the moon," remarked Anaïs Nin with considerable disinterest, after the lunar landing. "He has so much further to go within himself."

Yes, I know that Nin was talking about not the physical body but the psyche, but what I mean to suggest (the experience of fasting might be perfect proof) is that those two poles may not be so far apart after all, in fact may not even be different things, at least not in the way we think about them.

The body changes and shifts, goes through its seasons, over the span of its life.

My notebook of two years ago drifts, a trail of consciousness, a record of a person who doesn't exist anymore.

But also (of course) does.

The self and the self-that-was, or the self-that-will-be: all planets revolving around the same sun?

Which is the sun and which the planet?

One of the realizations I wrote about in that old notebook that rises to the surface always: that the fasting month, based on the lunar calendar, moves backward and backward in position across the calendar in successive years because the annual lunar cycle is ten days shorter than the annual solar cycle.

Ten years ago, the last time my mother and I fasted each day together, I was living in Buffalo, New York, and Ramadan was in the dead of winter.

When I did my very first fast, I was nine years old
and the fast was in July. Every thirty-six years you
revisit your old life through the fast. And throughout
your life the conditions and experiences of the fast
change.

This is like the inhale and the exhale, or like the
fast itself, which changes from the beginning of the
month through to the end of the month.

But honestly, doesn't the fast change during each
day? Sometimes easier, sometimes harder, but always
you have to bring your whole attention to fasting.

There is something about you that changes with
every minute, with every second, your physical body
refining and replacing itself in a constant state of
combustion.

And something about you that does not change.

How perfect then that the symbol for Ramadan,
the object in the sky that both begins and ends the
month of fasting, is the moon.

The moon that revolves around the earth and rotates
on its own axis at precisely the same speed. The only
heavenly object that rests with us in utter and eternal
equilibrium.

b *Sixth Day*

I find myself sleeping more. And eating less, even
when it is time to eat.

Rain is trickling down the gutter outside; the air is
a beautiful grey.

Why have I always—always—loved grey cloudy
days, rainy days even better, and not just summer
rain either, big warm drops splashing down; no,
I love as well the cold needling rain of spring and
the autumn drizzle so thick you can't feel it but
arrive home thoroughly soaked.

The soaking, I think: to be covered, suffused, bathed,
owned, by something you didn't even know was
around you.

I love the mysteries and the unexplainables. The
Kaaba—black house of God, called the Near
Mosque, circumambulated by millions, determin-
ing the direction of Muslim prayers, the cube at the
heart of the Masjid-e-Haram—is empty inside.

What does that emptiness mean?

When the prophet was taken on his *mehraj*, he
was taken first to the Far Mosque—Al-Aqsa, in

Jerusalem—and then into Heaven. Myriad events occurred there, but the final one was this: God changed the direction of prayers—from the Far Mosque in Jerusalem, to the Near Mosque in Mecca.

What does it mean? That you must worship what is closest to you? But the steed bore him to the Far Mosque first and thence into heaven, yes? So maybe Heaven, the physical (or metaphorical) site where God is supposed to be, is not really the most important point?

Revelation is handy: God whispering in your ears, smoothing out uncertainties, explaining what was supposed to happen next. But what do you do when you are an ordinary mortal, in doubt, hearing nothing but silence?

At any rate, there has always been a lively debate over the real location of the Far Mosque, defined in scripture not geographically but solely by that adjective, "far." Rumi put his two cents in when he wrote, "That mosque Sulayman built was not made of bricks and stone. The farthest mosque is the one inside you."

Besides the way that Rumi, preeminent Sufi teacher, sounds quite like a yogic sage here, it is also interesting that he makes no distinction between the destroyed Temple of Solomon, mourned by countless people, and the mosque that was built in its place.

What if every mosque and synagogue were the same place? Worshipped in by different communities with their own litanies and liturgies and scriptures, at their own appointed times? If only.

And why is the Kaaba so important? Because there a black stone fell from the sky? Because Ibrahim and Ismail built it as a house of worship—but why there? What happened there?

There in the desert, as her infant son Ismail was dying, Hajira, first wife of Ibrahim, put her son down and ran in the desert to look for water.

Looking for water in the desert? What was she thinking?

For a moment, her son dying in her arms, she panicked.

I think this is the true definition of faith: In his almost-death, Ismail found life. Where his heels hammered the ground a spring issued forth. He drank.

Meanwhile Hajira in her panic ran by him several more times before seeing that he had already been saved.

Is "heaven," or our idea of what that place is, relevant to spiritual practice? Here's one answer: During the *Hajj*, when pilgrims commemorate Hajira's search for water, they do not stop when and where the water burst forth; instead they run between the two hills Safa and Marwa seven times—the number of times Hajira is said to have run before she noticed the spring water.

Which had been there all along, though underground.

The Kaaba is a sacred place because it is the place a person refused to believe the most horrifying possibility: That she had been abandoned. That she was alone in the desert without succour. That there was nothing she could do to save her baby.

And there, the closest object to the Near Mosque, the sole object—since the Mosque is empty inside—at the heart of Islam is the tomb of Hajira, the tomb of a woman, an African woman who heard nothing in her ears but the beating of her blood and the most illogical of thoughts:

The boy is dying. *Run.*

LATE AFTERNOON

We're layered backward in time. Choices made last night, last year, or ten years ago braid us together toward the exact moment, the exact place we now find ourselves.

It's harder for me to think about this process as karma—every action accreting consequences—than to think about it as *kismet*. Kismet is "fate," but only in a sense. It's a fate that's governed by a myriad, a million different actions and reactions throughout the universe, throughout time.

To think about this question simply: My body's exhaustion now is the product, perhaps, of not eating quite enough this morning. Whatever calories and vitamins I ingested at 5:00 a.m. interacted in all kinds of chemical processes throughout my body and have affected my mood, my energy level, my ability to perceive the world around me.

Yet I am not solely governed by physical fate, am I? There is a yoga class at 7 p.m. I really want to go. I'll go if I don't manage to talk myself out of going.

Also this afternoon for the first time (I am sure not for the last), I felt sad. I wanted the fast to be over, so I could just make a cup of coffee, go into my writing room and work. And classes start next week; how will I manage?

I wander around the house, distracted, unable to fix myself to any one task. I am slow on the uptake, have communication difficulties with everyone. I chose the fast for myself but dozens of people around me are affected by how I interact with them.

We hope that we only exert positive energies on others. Kismet after all cuts both ways: Our fates are woven, but each of us is one of a multiple million weavers, all separate from a million (billion? or more?) other beings.

The refractions of our actions through space and time are literally endless.

Fasting is a physical practice of course. If my mind cannot fix on the tasks that need to be completed—syllabi to be finalized, a manuscript of essays due to the publisher on August 31—at least my body can concentrate on the fast.

Told to breathe.

In the late afternoon of the sixth day I dreamed the fast to be over. But I'm not yet even through a quarter of the month, not yet through even one phase of the moon.

7 Seventh Day

One time.

When you say "One time," in a story, you mean a
time that happened in the past, but one you are still
living in, living at that very moment. How often
have you caught a whiff of patchouli, seen someone
wearing a yellow scarf, heard the Indigo Girls singing
"Love's Recovery"—and suddenly you are gone, out
of the present, backward in time, some other place,
miles away, how easy it is to be transported, how
slight our connection to our body is, as an entity in
space.

The fast is a permanent "one time," because you are
disconnected from the physical network of food
and exchange of mass and matter that connects all
the physical universe. You are a mere ghost, hover-
ing, breathing the air in and out, not partaking, but
affecting the world nonetheless with your karmic
actions, even with your breathing.

This morning there was the same thick rain I
dreamed about yesterday. Then the sun came up and
everything was warm and gold. By now the sun's

light has whitened, covered by thin clouds. A cool breeze ruffles through the trees.

Three moods in one day.

So it is all right for me to feel glorious, glum, and content, one after the other, sometimes all at once.

Why am I always reaching? For the next thing and the next thing?

Isn't this one moment all I have?

But, "This one time . . ."

I don't, after all, believe that this life is the only life I have. Not just that there is a life before this one, and a life after this one, and maybe another one after that, and another after that. No, that idea is just scripture, whether in the Bhagavad Gītā, which speaks in terms of reincarnation, or in the Quran or Bible, which speak in terms of afterlife.

No, what I mean is a multiple million possibilities of life happening right now. The me who woke up late and didn't fast today. The me who decided not to move to Oberlin after all. The me who never went to New York. The me who didn't switch his major in college and continued to study politics and went on to go to law school.

Where did all those Kazims end up? Are they happy? Though I am content with my life at the present moment and wish for no other, I supremely hope that no matter what choices I made I would still have found happiness.

And if this is the case, does that mean our happiness does not depend on our physical condition or our temporary state of well-being; that it comes from another source?

I know this much: I can only live my own life, live it truly, trying always to make "one time" now.

Should all the multiple possibilities, all the different paths, be this one, my one life, at this moment?

Olga Broumas wrote that some sects of Hasidic Jews teach that sin is an act of divided intention.

Similarly in yoga practice you are trying to learn to see things as they really are, free of your past preconceptions.

And in Islam it is intention, even more than action, that determines the karma, or fatal effect, of any given action.

Our tendency to live in terms of "one time," distant from our present condition, always thinking about something else, either looking backward or looking forward, may have some relationship to the animal fear of being alarmingly present in the corporeal body.

Because to be really present in the body, to breathe in it, to use it, to stretch it and feel it, and not just once, but over the course of weeks or months or years, to feel it age, to know its character, is to know: that the body dies.

To be in hunger. To look at everything as if you have never seen it before. To speak to people as if you have never tried to speak. To move the body without inflow of energy, to try in the late afternoon, as you deplete and deplete, to do physical tasks: This is to know how the body can fail.

And how the body lives through that failure.

Walking through my house in the early evening, like a ghost, picking up my cat and kissing him on the head, hanging a jacket on the hook. A body that doesn't even know it is moving.

You get the feeling then at that moment, the light outside dimming to rich blue, that the body is not really you, but also that it is you and more.

I was running this morning in the darkness again. I came to a place where the streetlights were out, the patch of darkness where before I had thought about death. I looked down at the street where I had seen the streaks of tar that resembled Arabic letters. I looked more carefully. In fact, there, curled up in the streaks of the tar—one of the workers must have used a dispenser—there was writing in English.

In the pre-dawn, running before hunger, I read: "one time."

My "one time" is now. Right now. My body is alive. And singing.

EVENING

The sky has opened and is pouring rain down in a solid mass of water.

We say "has opened" as if the sky is a solid mass but it isn't.

Or is it?

Isn't the sky solid, full of particles and molecules and atoms?

Maybe the body is like the sky, not a corporeal individual after all, but merely a locus, a space in which phenomena occur.

I'm reading books about alternative bodies.

Waking by Matthew Sanford is about his experience coming back to his body through yoga after a horrific car accident that killed his father and sister and paralyzed Matthew himself. He writes at the beginning, "I know what it feels like to leave my body." His life was his journey back to that body.

Eavesdropping by Stephen Kuusisto describes his experiences as a blind person learning to listen to the world.

People in other bodies move through entire universes I know nothing about.

The body is in transition, never a static place. Both Sanford's and Kuusisto's memoirs are titled with participles—verbs of action for bodies in action.

Water in the earth sinks deep, then emerges into plants and trees, flows out and is drunk by us and returns, evaporates, condenses—water, rain, rivers, all in constant motion.

The sky too is like this, gasses forming and reforming, carbon going into and out of the atmosphere.

The body is like this too.

We, like all of our planetary systems, are in imbalance. Water is being used up quicker than can be replenished. More carbon is going into the air than is coming out.

What will happen to our bodies—our own human, individual bodies: touch yours now, right now, touch the skin, it is real—what happens to our bodies next?

And next?

8 *Eighth Day*

LATE AFTERNOON

Yesterday as I got off my bike and was about to climb the short set of steps to our front porch, I noticed a spider, not small, suspended in the middle of the wide stairs. I looked up to see if she was hanging from a branch of the flowering dogwood that dominates our front yard, the tree the previous owners of the house planted in memory of Martin Luther King, Jr.

But above me, clear to the grey sky. Where was the spider hanging from? What was she connected to? I went to the left of her and as I walked up the stairs, I felt the sticky strand of web across my face, my hands. She trailed after me, floating in thin air, bound by the web between us.

I know that there are people reading my online account of fasting because there are comments below my postings, and because people email me to tell me that they have been reading. This is not at all like in 2007, when I wrote privately in my notebook, a notebook that until now I have only showed to three other people.

This writing feels like secret writing, but is the most unsecret of all. The other day my mother, home from a pilgrimage to the Middle East, told me that she was reading also. All along I have worried about being alone, but in this strange incorporeal space, I find myself connected to numbers and numbers of other beings.

The blankness of the day, of the wall in front of me, or in this case of the screen, makes my online Ramadan journal a very different experience than inscribing words onto paper, a physical expression that cannot be transmitted universally, only shared body by body.

But perhaps this is a better demonstration of the difference between body and spirit. These are not different matters at all, not opposites, one not mortal and the other immortal; rather they are each different methods of transmission of the same essence, our true inner natures, for which we haven't yet found an adequate word, and perhaps it's best that way.

Truth should be wordless.

In the spirit of this community, of this house where I now live and where its builders lived for fifty-four years, and where the people to whom they sold it lived for forty-four years after that, I have invited students and friends to come each Friday during Ramadan and have fast-breaking dinner with me.

Last night I cooked and cooked—rice and salad and *chole*, my own secret recipe! I had no idea who was coming, as I had issued the open invitation. I assumed that whomever came would be my guest.

But what if I had no guests? I had to prepare anyhow. You do not know what is going to happen.

Right when you think there's no one, there's someone. Right when you think there's someone, there's no one.

The spider hanging in the doorway floated behind me.

Fasting is a secret it is hard to tell.

Ninth Day

At the end of the day in the silence and quiet.

Today I was around food a lot, but had no appetite.

You are not supposed to tempt yourself in the fast.

Because it is not a game, perhaps. Remembering Gandhi's *brahmacharya* experiments. *Brahmacharya*, traditionally interpreted as "chastity," now is commonly translated as "right conduct."

Because "right conduct," conduct that does not cause harm to others, cannot be limited to the single sphere of sexual behavior or to restrictions of any one kind.

For example, a fast from eating.

Because in the fast you are also not supposed to: raise your voice, get overly emotional, talk badly about other people, gossip, engage in violence of any kind, smoke, take drugs, or swear or talk coarsely.

In other words, your relationship to the community and world around you has to switch from contesting and confrontation to acceptance and receptiveness.

It's not that I've lost my appetite for food, but I find myself craving whole and healthy foods like brown rice, fruits, beans, and kale.

There are two huge squashes on the counter that came from our garden. I want to slice them very thin and then make a curry with them.

In a fast, one changes one's relationship to pleasure.

Is pleasure merely instantaneous, on the surface, with only one experience in each—for example, in the taste of squash curry?.

Or does the pleasure penetrate all the various levels in the body? Does the food continue to give pleasure at every stage of the body's process of eating? Taste, digestion, and egestion, and then afterward the ways the food that was taken in builds the body.

I know I would always laugh when we would learn yoga poses that were supposed to aid with expelling matter from the body, but honestly: Isn't how food leaves the body at least as important as how it enters the body?

Just like in the film *The Matrix*, our bodies really are little processing plants for the physical matter of the earth and the universe.

Maybe the mind and what the mind thinks and how the mind speaks is also like this.

Contributing to or impeding the well-being of all creatures in the world.

You free yourself from food during the day but then you are supposed to eat at night. You free yourself from food, maybe, so you can actually and truly experience that food.

When I ate a tomato, warm off the plant, in Santa Cruz, California, in September 2004, I tasted the first real tomato in my life.

Same for the white peach I ate, orchard-warm, on the island of Corsica, in July 2000. First peach of my life.

Purifying the spirit in an impure body is a tough challenge.

Purifying the body with our current food production and distribution system seems impossible. Fruits and vegetables are driven thousands of miles across the country and taste nothing like themselves upon delivery to massive grocery stores.

And anyone who really knew where factory meat and milk came from wouldn't want to eat or drink these.

Visit the website www.themeatrix.com to see what I mean.

Maybe *brahmacharya* should extend to our treatment of animals: Imagine if we ceased manipulating their sexual practices by technology in order to produce milk and flesh for our consumption.

We have an opportunity now to understand our body as a little ecosystem with its own environmental crisis going on. What we've done to the outside we've also done to the inside.

I do not think we will be able to fix one without fixing the other.

10 *Tenth Day*

Twice recently, in the evening after eating, people have remarked on my physical condition, saying I looked "tired" or "frail."

First reaction: Hackles up, because we all want to be strong.

Second reaction: Interest, because during the fast I do feel tired or frail, but these comments both came after I had eaten.

The second time I was told that I looked tired I *was* feeling tired. Not because I had been fasting. I was tired because I had been eating.

The sunlight is lying across the road outside in a vertical stripe. The leaves of the big white flowering dogwood—the one planted for Martin Luther King, Jr.—are bit by bit turning red.

Bodies and trees change, sure, but roads do as well. I saw it. Last year when we were looking for houses we went to see an 1860s-era farmhouse on the edge of town. The owner was taking us into the backyard behind the barn and there were these big slabs of flat stone making a path on the property.

"That used to be College Street," she said, gesturing to them. "Those are the old stones. The previous owner bought them and brought them here when they repaved the road for cars."

Every piece of matter moves, whether by human design or not, and we are in an eternal process of shifting molecules around, one from the other. Streets shed their skins; humans do as well.

When you stoke a fire—by eating, for example—the fire burns hotter, faster.

It can tire you out.

And fasting isn't about denial anyhow, nor about severing a connection between mind and spirit.

The experience of fasting is really the opposite: playing with that boundary, exploring the relationship with an individual mind, the spiritual substance of the body and the material, incarnate locus of that awareness.

One fasts in order to know the outlines and limits of that material-spiritual connection.

After all, if everything is moving at different speeds the farther away from the individual body you get, then perhaps somewhere inside—a deep somewhere— there is a place that is barely moving at all.

First day of classes. Today I meet my new students. We'll transfer thoughts, ideas, theories, fictions, and poems between us.

At the end of each semester I always tell my classes, "This might be the last time in our lifetimes that we are all together in one room at the same time, talking about literature." I'm probably right about that, but someone always gasps in horror.

And that someone is probably also right. Why mark the signs of impermanence and intransience? We think we need to be reminded—and perhaps we do—but we oughtn't. We need only look down at our own hands, feel our bodies under our palms.

All bodies are frail. All bodies are weak, or are a wink away from weakness, from age, from diminishing ability.

There is a rule, a rule of all matter in the universe, not just the fleshly human one:

We love the garden, it is heaven, but we cannot stay.

11 *Eleventh Day*

LATE MORNING

I know I am in trouble today. I didn't eat enough solid food this morning. I started with miso soup. It is not a good idea to eat soup or drink smoothies in the morning because they fill you up.

What you need for a day of fasting is complex carbohydrates, preferably whole foods like brown rice, quinoa, or other whole grains; also protein, and also fat. I ate some fruit and yogurt but I ought to have had more legumes—what's in the miso isn't really enough.

You also need enough fiber to keep everything moving through, because without much food your digestive system doesn't get the practice it needs.

I did drink water at the end of the morning meal, but once again I drank too fast, so I haven't been able to keep much of it in my body.

Well, each day of the fast ought to be different, right? Not to be so easy that all you're doing is skipping lunch?

While it is incorrect to put the body into discomfort during a fast—by exerting yourself, by tempting yourself needlessly—you are meant to feel under duress. A controlled situation.

On most days I've been careful to supply myself with enough nutrition, but I also want to offer myself treats.

Coffee was the hardest to go without—coffee, my dream, my rapture—what else could I do during a long, autumn afternoon, but sit with a notebook, drink coffee, and write sentences?

All my books of prose—two novels and a queer autobiography—I wrote in sentences, line by line, not knowing where they were going to lead, not knowing who the characters were, what the plot was, when I would end. The sentences of my first novel, *Quinn's Passage*, never wove together. They still flutter, in the wind, the sound of waves crashing on the shore in the background.

Eventually the autobiography organized itself, and quite neatly. The second novel took much, much longer, and the threads and plots wove together more by instinct than by design.

During the fast I haven't much been able to write, though I have two deadlines, one for a book of essays that I am supposed to turn over to the publisher as of yesterday, the other for a translation of a Marguerite Duras novel, a novel that also takes place at the seashore, the waves likewise crashing into the characters' ears.

As in *Quinn's Passage*, these characters live as if in dream space. You spend the whole novel submerged in their poetry, wondering if they will ever come to.

I drift between my external physical life and this submerged interior life throughout the day. Does the fast help me focus on one or the other at any given moment? I want to say not so far, but maybe in small instants fasting does. For a second or two I get it, then I'm just hungry or want to take a nap or watch a movie or provide myself with some other distraction.

I did teach a writing class yesterday and will teach another one tonight. In between these, I taught a yoga class this morning, to a student who had never done yoga before. I thought, how wonderful—to be at the beginning of something.

As at the beginning of the day, before the sun rises, when I run. When not fasting I used to run in the afternoon—after coffee, after writing, the mental activity still buzzing in brain, I would hit the road.

I do have a little jar of instant decaf coffee. Decaf, because at night is when I want to drink coffee now.

True coffee feels too harsh on the stomach early in the morning. Instant, for two reasons: first because it's fast to make.

But second—the real reason, the true reason: I like the way instant coffee tastes. When I was growing up, we never had ground coffee, only instant, which is what my parents always drank. It's comfort food for me, a way of being with them.

These experiences that feel connected—coffee, writing, yoga, running, teaching—have all transformed and moved into different relationships with each other during this month of fasting. My whole life is in more or less tumult because of the fast, both physically and emotionally.

When you see a person who is fasting you think you are seeing someone who is refraining, restraining, but really you are seeing a whole whirlwind of both mental and physical activity.

12 _Twelfth Day_

EARLY EVENING

Tonight I am cooking for a small and impromptu group of people, my favorite kind of gathering. One that just happens.

Last week on the way home from yoga class I asked my friend Doris, who is also my yoga teacher, if she wanted to come over for dinner. She said, "You should come over, we are making omelets!"

So we went two houses down to Doris's house and had omelets.

This is how I grew up, going from one house—23 Harmony Cove—to another—168 Sterling Avenue—several times during the day, eating breakfast at one house, lunch at the other, playing in the yard of whichever house I happened to be at.

And neither of these houses was my parents' house. One belonged to my uncle, the other to my aunt. We lived far away from Winnipeg in the northern part of Manitoba in a town called Jenpeg, which I am not sure exists anymore.

Though I've discovered there is a Facebook group for people who used to live in Jenpeg.

The Internet is bringing back—at least in simulation or simulacrum—things that don't exist anymore.

This morning as I walked around the house doing chores, I left the front door open, the screen door closed, like we did in the houses of my childhood. 317 River Road. 93 Wilcox. 28 Ranch Trail West.

Ironically I cannot remember our Jenpeg address. That is if we had one, in such a small town.

I do feel like I am suspended in time between places, not really knowing where I am or what I am supposed to be doing.

Tonight, in a few minutes really, I am supposed to be going to a welcome reception on campus. It is always strange, when fasting, to stand in a room full of people who are sipping sodas or nibbling on a snack.

As strange as cooking for a group, cooking food you yourself haven't actually tasted.

But you cook for them, you are with them, because so separated from the world, all you want to do is love.

Today I was sitting in a large meeting of the general faculty. New faculty members were being introduced. When their names were called, they would rise so we could see them and greet them.

Oddly, every time someone's name was called I
found myself wanting to wave my hand and say,
"I'm over here!"

13 Thirteenth Day

EARLY EVENING

This morning Doris came to our house for yoga. We rolled out our mats in the gabled room on the third floor, the one I want to paint bright orange but that Marco wants to paint light blue.

Perhaps one wall orange and one wall blue?

Orange is the color of the sixth chakra, the one that governs creativity, expressiveness, sexuality.

Orange is one of my favorite colors and I know it well from my years of traveling by air, my years of being selected for the "random searches."

The terror threat advisory has been "raised" to orange, we are told. But really it's been at orange for eight years. The day after the inauguration, it was lowered to yellow and I nearly wept.

Though returned to orange it has.

Orange the little fruit I peeled open this morning. Orange the sun on the horizon as it sets.

Orange alert means now is the time for creative expression, for flowering; now is the time, more than any other, to eschew practices of exhaustion and death and turn toward our interior sources of love and light.

Outside the window I catch sight of Doris walking her dog. Other friends of ours stop by on their bike ride and have some tea.

I like when people gather around. I believe that art and art-making can be part of this community-building and peace-making practice, which it is essential we undertake at this historical moment.

After yoga I spent all day making final adjustments to a manuscript of essays on poetry and art called *Orange Alert.*

Orange alert, because as my hunger can be directed to a more focused practice of yoga and of writing, I think our capacity for positive action outweighs our destructiveness, but we're never going to find this out until we empty ourselves and look.

The leaves of the dogwood are turning orange. Which means the earth is swinging around the sun; each day the time until fast-breaking shortens by two minutes because the days are getting shorter and shorter.

Fire that summit of orange can nurture or combust.

A body that eats food burns food all day long and requires more.

A body that fasts has to learn a new way, to sustain its energy and nurture itself; the fasting body cannot burn because it becomes dimly aware that the better you burn the faster you burn, and that when you burn you must create more and more fire.

And if the only way you know how to live is by burning, then at the end all you will have left is ash.

 *Fourteenth Day*

LATE AFTERNOON

Yellow-gold light of late afternoon: my favorite light.

I didn't have time to be hungry today. All morning I worked on the Duras translation, hearing the surge of sentences echoing in the expanse of space in which the novel takes place—a beach, with the sky and the ocean nearly indistinguishable.

Does the fast become a way to separate oneself, uncouple from the world-as-it-is?

Or can you use the opportunity to come closer to others?

Tonight I am preparing an *iftar* for some students and have also invited some friends and colleagues to join us.

Once again I do not know quite how many people will be coming, or whom they will be.

But I don't know who I myself am really, do I?

In the middle of the day, there are *Jummah* prayers in the student center. One of the professors offers a *khutba* and then leads the *Jummah* prayers.

Jummah (which means, prosaically, Friday) is a prayer that is supposed to be performed with the community. This enjoinment made sense, since Islam was otherwise such an individual religion.

I've never been a big fan of the group prayer, which usually goes too fast for me. I like to linger over the Arabic syllables, stay a long time in the postures (which remind me so much of the *surya-namaskar* you would do in a yoga class), and besides I haven't been very good at keeping up my daily prayers.

Although that's odd, because the daily prayers are an easy practice whereas the month of fasting is arduous, yet I have chosen that more difficult practice to be faithful to.

Is this because I think I have something to prove?

At any rate, I haven't prayed *Jummah* for probably fifteen years.

I have a hard time with prayer because when I pray I want to believe god will see me.

But since I am not sure what the nature of god is (or God if you prefer, or G–D, or whatever) I don't know how I can speak.

Somewhat like speaking out loud to an empty room hoping like anything you are overheard.

There was one prayer I offered; I couldn't resist the urge to.

In the summer of 2008 I had gone to Al-Andalus, the Muslim south of Spain. There in the Cathedral of Córdoba, I found myself needing to pray.

The reason is that the Cathedral used to be the (unspeakably huge) Mezquita, Córdoba's Mosque. When the kingdom fell to the Catholic monarchs of the north, the building was given to the Catholic Church, who consecrated the site and built a full-size sixteenth-century cathedral inside.

That should give you an idea about how big the Mezquita is.

Because since its earliest days the building had been shared by the Christian and Muslim communities of Córdoba (until the Muslim community became too large, and they bought out the Christian community, giving them money to build a church in another location), my friends thought I ought to be able to pray there. The security guard said no, this was not permitted.

So there I was, a vexed Muslim in a vexed Mosque. It was the only place in the world I had a desire to pray, and of all the Muslims in that building, wandering around like tourists in their own house, I felt I was the only one who could.

And so I did.

Today when I saw the notice about the *Jummah* prayer on campus, I thought to myself: I should go.

And then immediately after that I thought: Why would I go?

I feel such a personal relationship with my beliefs, never wanting to explain them to anyone, and I feel so out of sorts with the community-at-large that a communal offering is the last place I wanted to put myself.

Yet I am putting myself in it tonight, aren't I? But that's on my terms: with food I am preparing, I am offering, and in my own home.

Is my spiritual practice always on my own terms? I know that's not true, because I can remember all the times in yoga class when I wanted to quit and give up, especially in a difficult posture, and I would tell myself, "This is your small ego that wants to prevent you from an experience you need to have. Stay here. Stay now."

Maybe there is divinity in the energy and grace that moves between bodies and within them. In which case I am inviting god or an idea of god into my house tonight.

So this afternoon I went, humbly, to the makeshift mosque on the second floor of the student union.

My friend Ali, who leads the prayers, was beside himself with pleasure that I had come. When we lined up for prayers behind him, the students and I, we were the same, bareheaded, barefoot, the same.

I let my hands drop at my sides, since I am Shi'a, while the other students folded their hands across their abdomens, the posture that Sunni Muslims use for prayers.

I also noticed the two women who laid their rugs behind the row of men. I wished this could be different, that we could be interspersed, and if not interspersed then in the same line.

Everything isn't equal in the room, I thought to myself as I recited verses quietly to myself, but here I am, at least, here I am.

15 *Fifteenth Day*

NIGHT

I find it delicious when I change my mind.

Because to change your mind means to be open to the possibilities of the infinite paths.

True that fasting is an internal process, but the fast can come to fruition amongst others as well.

For example, the month of Ramzan in 1998 when I was living at home with my parents and I woke every day with my mother to eat, then fasted with her throughout the month.

Last night the students from the Muslim Student Association came for *iftar*. Seven students came and there were eight others, faculty and staff from the college, plus the people I live with.

It was a joy to break my fast with others but also to provide food for everyone, food I myself had prepared without having tasted it.

Each Friday I hold a fast-breaking dinner, and because of their experiences participating in the dinner last night, two people, a friend and one of the people I live with, both decided that on Friday they would fast for the day so at the evening meal they also would be able to break their fasts.

My housemate will wake up tomorrow morning to fast with me, so for the first time since the month began I will be fasting with another.

Tonight also we had dinner with friends, shared food and conversation. They were interested in my experiences fasting, what it was like, what the point and purpose is.

Fasting isn't about "atonement," I explained to them. It is more for the purpose of focusing the mind on spiritual practices rather than the less subtle requirements of the body.

Though all the metaphors for spiritual enlightenment and for mental advances seem to be metaphors of the body. To "ascend." To "see clearly."

Earlier in the day our neighbors came over and we went into what I now call "the practice room" and we all four of us did yoga together.

It occurred to me during the meal that this is what we all want—a sense of fellowship and community with like-minded people.

We choose our community because they help us and support us, not always in ways we expect.

I call that room on the third floor of our house "the practice room" because various spiritual practices occur there, including yoga, zen meditation, and for the first time on Friday, *salaat*, or Muslim prayer.

Three of the students who came for *iftar* asked me if there was a place where they could pray. I did not hesitate to lead them to the room where meditation and yoga take place, my immediate action revealing to me what I had paid lip service to, all along—that yoga was for me a form of prayer.

When we went up there I immediately crossed to the makeshift altar and removed the small figures of Ganesh and Buddha. "We also do meditation and yoga here; that's why you see Ganesh and Buddha," I told the students.

I wonder why I felt the responsibility to explain myself, I who am fasting, who am offering *iftar* to the students, providing a place for them to pray and prayer rugs as well.

The icons on the altar are not objects of worship, rather they are arrows pointing in a certain direction.

And I am a man with many arrows inside me, each pointing in a different direction.

I suppose I may need help pulling them out, but
I am not sure that bearing them all isn't part of
what's happening to me in this life.

I could count up my unspeakable blessings, but the
guests have gone and it is time to wash the dishes.

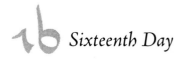 *Sixteenth Day*

MIDAFTERNOON

The blankness of a mind or month.

Month meaning moon or mouth.

Moon not blank of course but marked by many passing objects.

Blank in that the dreams or fears of millenia are written on it.

Moon that has no light of its own.

Each Friday the observatory here in town has open hours. I always want to go on the full moon, but my friend Dan who is an astronomer tells me it's no good to look at the moon when it is full.

Full moons being too bright. *Success in Circuit lies*—

My mouth blank then as the full moon passes, marking the halfway point through the month of fasting.

We wind down now, we reach further both into ourselves and outward to those around us.

A double motion, equal intensity, both at once.

As in yoga postures—open and contract, match inhale for exhale. Make the breath even.

No space marking delineation between inhale and exhale, one shifting in to the other.

Who was it who said God lives between the inhale and the exhale?

If that is an eddying and swirling place—like the Hudson River estuary, which swirls and heads back to the ocean—then where do we look for ourselves?

It's a sacred month, regardless of fasting, because it is said to be the month in which the revelation of the Quran began.

When Gabriel came to the prophet in the cave and said, "Read. Read in the name of the One who created you, made you from a clot of blood."

And what night of the month was that? Complicated question.

Supposedly: An odd-numbered night in the third week of the month. Cryptic.

So most people repeat the prayers and rituals associated with this night—*Lail-ut-al-Qadr*—on three different nights, the nineteenth, the twenty-first, and the twenty-third of Ramzan.

Sounds crazy but also beautiful. You say the prayers three times because you don't know which night is which.

Or as I wrote in a poem called "Ramadan," *You will never know which night's mouth is sacredly reciting/ and which night's recitation is secretly mere wind.*

And the month winds down as well in secret. Last night at dinner one of my friends asked, When do you have to stop fasting?

And I had to explain—the month is not over, Eid does not come, until the first sliver of the new moon is sighted in the sky.

A table of blank faces.

The month had a secret beginning, a secret night in the middle, and a secret end.

Maybe this month is not an actual unit of chronological time but a form of metaphor.

And what if it doesn't matter, which actual night the revelation happened? Maybe the point is that it occurs every night.

Maybe the moon and the sun only hang in the sky to explain something to us.

Maybe the mouth also, the cells and organs of the
body, our bones and muscles, the way we eat and
drink and breathe and live, maybe all of these are
lines of verse, looping script in the darkness, which
we still have to learn how to read.

Seventeenth Day

Rain outside, the world a deep gray-green, each color leaning toward the other.

Objects in the world that become the other: Breath (inhale and exhale). Light (night travels through twilight to day and the other way as well). Bodies. Plants. Of course even the stone sloughs off into space with a touch or a million million touches.

Draw closer to your sources the things that mark you as a participant in creation, made of its constituent parts, the ingredients of the universe. Draw close to the moments of exchange of physical matter, and also the exchange of spiritual kindness and energy.

Last night I watched a Taiko drumming performance. The drummers were so passionate and physically connected to the movements they were making, gesturing and chanting verses as they struck the drums. The drum almost seemed part of the body that was sounding; or a better explanation is that the body of the drummer itself becomes part of the drum.

We think that there is a division between body (physical matter of the self, skin and bones, hair and blood), mind (sense-making organ, the thing you think you mean when you say "I") and the spirit (the actual third thing, the real internal self, beyond the physical changes of the corporeal body and the fluctuations of the consciousness).

And if we think there is a division then perhaps we think the body is temporal, that it disappears, cycles back into creation, while the mind and the spirit are the immortal parts that transcend.

You think something different when you are living in a body that fasts, that removes itself from the cycle of matter transference (food and water) and instead depends, for a time, on energy transference only (breath).

You imagine the equation is different, that the spirit resides in both the mind and the body equally. That both have their version of temporality and immortality. That it takes knowing one to know the other and takes knowing the other to know the third.

That understanding the self is also a cyclical process, the way food energy enters the body, the body itself changes and regenerates, enters and re-enters the matrix of creation.

Water pouring from the air into the ground. We are breathing some also. It will fill the plants and trees and the squash in the garden and return to us eventually.

I have a particular love of sudden storms, of racing for the top floors to close all the windows.

Your house is something you have to take care of for the sake of all the beings within.

Your body is like that also.

18 *Eighteenth Day*

NIGHT

We cross so many borders in our lives. Not just in my case from England to Canada and then Canada to the United States, but crossing from one region of life to another.

In each place, you are an immigrant, without papers.

I decided to translate a Duras novel because I wanted to know what was going to happen next.

But what happens next to me? The plot of a fast is easy: You are supposed to eat at a certain time in the morning, you restrain from eating during certain hours, and then at a certain moment you eat again.

But the plot of a life? Especially my life—all unwritten, no guide to what should happen to me.

I find myself fixed in locality during the fast. First of all because I don't want to expend much energy by going anywhere, but when I do leave the house to go to my office or to town to run errands, every place means more.

Perhaps because I am moving so slowly through?

Plot in my first novel *Quinn's Passage* is incidental. Quinn is at a beach town. Some things happen, he meets a few people. The story is episodic, and the episodes have sequence but no consequence except internal emotional consequence.

Plot in my second novel *The Disappearance of Seth* is accidental—events take on significance precisely because everything is consequential; events call to mind other events, sometimes separated by years and continents. The characters' lives are explored through association, layering of memory and experiences, and their brief and tenuous and on occasion unremembered interactions with one another. In that sense the novel could be considered an essay—a fictional essay—on the nature of history.

If the plot of my life is writing then I have nothing but time.

Hours today, going over the translation of the weird Duras novel about the beach and the deserted town.

Remembering the times I was writing the novels or writing *Bright Felon*, how hours would be spent making sentences.

Individual poems and essays are different for me; they are a part of my normal life; one doesn't have to be a monk to take part in them. But a novel or a book-length project is like a big cup of water you have to drink before beginning the fast.

And finishing writing—knowing you are at the end of such a project—is like crossing a border as well, seeking asylum. You come into the country without any of your belongings, quite unaware of the customs or language of the new place in which you find yourself.

Day eighteen of the fast, I lie on the couch in the middle afternoon, a little tired of it all. Wishing I could just have a sandwich and a cup of coffee and get back to work.

Also, I feel for the first time I have really sabotaged myself by not drinking enough water. I felt so under the weather that I think I might get sick from dehydration and have to break my fast.

Intentionally breaking the fast without good reason incurs severe penalties: One is supposed to make up the fast, but also one is supposed to pay for the release of a certain number of captives or enslaved people.

I always wondered if that penalty was a metaphor, but whether metaphorical or not it is a testament to the intended egalitarianism of the Islamic faith.

I calm myself down a little bit by trying to move more slowly, not think too hard, not get excited or impatient about anything.

Of course I always fail at anything important. It feels essential that I fail. And so must release whatever I have enslaved; held captive.

What if I let go of the desire to fail and allowed myself to come to fruition?

Fruition with twelve days yet to fast?

What happens after I cease failing?

19 *Nineteenth Day*

PREDAWN

On Friday I am supposed to read a poem at a multi-faith investiture ceremony for the director of the office of spiritual life at the college.

It's a difficult task because as always, I am not sure what I myself believe.

Neither about the spiritual nature of the universe, nor about the nature of the spiritual path.

Does the path—so important that it is discussed in the very first chapter of the Quran, considered to be the condensation of all of its multiple meanings—require solitary pursuit or can a community take part?

Certainly for me the path has always been a lonely walk only because I haven't often found partners who believed what I believed.

Challenging of course, since as I mentioned I am always changing my mind.

Is the relationship between Creator and Creation a constant feedback loop, like the water falling out of the sky, which suffuses all matter and then returns skyward?

Or does energy flow out in a great exhale, ultimately—one would suspect—to flow back in to Somewhere, like the star-matter of the universe hurtling outward from the Big Bang in what must still be the first half of existence?

Or is there some third or fourth or fifth model for what we actually are, where we came from, where we're going?

The one truth I seem to be agreed upon (agreed upon with whom? myself? my Self?) is that "this"—this moment, this existence, this world, this universe—can't be "all there is."

Or can it?

It is easy in the predawn, before the sun has returned, as you receive proof once again of the circular nature of existence, to say what you believe or disbelieve, to fess up to your gray areas and your doubts.

Is it possible to bring this exploration into the light of day, possible to bring the very individual questions of the smallest shard of eternity—a single human body—into the public space of the community, possible to express the taxonomy of confusion in the forum of ritual and ceremony?

I've always thought of a poem as an open door.

"Welcome and entertain any guests, even if they are a horde of barbarians that sweep your house clean of its furniture," said Rumi. "Each has been sent as a guide from beyond."

I wonder if I will always be like this—unable to make up my mind. I wonder if this is my gift, to not know what I believe or think.

Maybe it is for others to "come to fruition" on day eighteen and spend another fortnight moving on to the next stage of awareness, or merely enjoying, or ignoring, what they have come to understand.

Maybe I just muddle through, learning nothing, and then begin again.

It certainly feels that way in my life. Or maybe fear holds me back. Fear that I'll really change and not be "myself" anymore.

For the moment, I don't know anything. About god, poetry, or people, three of the most important things in creation.

This realization is a version of a gift because it means I have to keep looking, keep thinking, keep feeling.

A couple of days ago I talked about myself as a man with a million arrows stuck in me.

Well, they are all pointing inside.

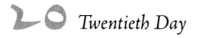 *Twentieth Day*

EARLY AFTERNOON

And so what if I can't figure it out, so what if I never figure it out?

Does it matter if the mind knows what oxygen is? The body still breathes.

And as for that thing some people call the "soul" or the "spirit" or in Sanskrit the *jivatman*, maybe it's not real in the first place; maybe the self is the marriage of the body and the mind, maybe there is no third thing.

Simplistic, I know. Because I know, from both Islam and my yoga practice, that intentional action is important, so important that punishment and rewards are often given based on intention rather than end result in both of these practices.

Perhaps I'll change my mind tomorrow, don't worry.

It is true, anyhow, that there are some for whom the path is through the mind, others for whom the path is through the body. Why argue if Margot Fonteyn, Albert Einstein, or Virginia Woolf was the greater genius when what they each did was so radically different?

In yoga there are numerous paths, that of *jñana* yoga, or yoga of knowledge, *bhakti* yoga, or yoga of devotion, *karma* yoga, or yoga of service and action, and even, yes, *hatha* yoga, a yoga of the body that seeks to understand the spirit through examination of the body and its attendant parts, which in the Yoga Sutras includes the mind.

The mind being an organ just like any other: skin, lungs, heart, spleen.

There are other yogas, an infinite number of paths, as there are an infinite number of people.

Yoga is not just for people who can afford mats, and who have a yoga studio nearby. Yoga is from the same Sanskrit word that gives the word "yolk." And "yoke."

And, interestingly: "religion."

Which can be both yolk and yoke, fruitfully and restrictively.

Yoga is a practice, not unlike fasting, that allows us to link the inside—the private experiences of the body and the mind—with the outside—the pulsing, breathing, actual world.

Fasting has made it easier for me to practice

vigorous *vinyasa* yoga. And though I am barely eating and worrying about losing muscular mass, fasting has made me stronger.

Today I attempted an arm balance that I had never tried before: From a forward bend take the hands through the legs and place them flat on the mat behind the heels. Tuck the shoulders behind the knees. Bend the arms and sit back high on the upper arms. Pressing into the ground and pulling the stomach in strongly, first shift the weight forward and then lift the feet off the ground. Extend the legs to straight.

Besides falling on my bottom and laughing in a mixture of delight and shame, I have never really gotten very far in this posture, whose Sanskrit name I do not know. But today, pulling my stomach in, I felt myself working with and against gravity, moving forward and back, up and down—I was not a body but a dynamic moment in time, an atom crashing against all the others, electrons twirling around me.

My arms felt strong enough, I expanded with breath and lifted my legs up and moved them toward straight.

And then I fell on my bottom.

With more delight than shame. But I also jammed my elbow as I fell, which hurt terribly, and after practice I iced it continuously with—having nothing else—a bag of frozen blackberries from the freezer. The elbow still feeling a little weakly.

I berate myself in all the old familiar ways: You come so far on a path and then you knock yourself back. You're no good at this anyhow. You'll never really be strong enough.

Partially those judgments ring true for me because I am not a natural yogi. I have an awkwardness in my body that's much more than skin deep. I've been practicing for ten years, and I meet people all the time who've practiced far less but are immeasurably more advanced in their *asana* practice.

Learning is a natural process, but very humbling always.

As a yoga teacher I have always viewed the limitations of my body as part of what I have to offer. Three years ago when I gained about twenty-five pounds and could barely do any of the binds or twists I used to do, I viewed this as a way of understanding my students, who maybe had never done yoga before, or never been physically active.

I hurt my elbow, but in this way I hope I can learn something about the posture, about my elbow, about how to best practice yoga with myself and with others.

The mind and the body have lots in common: they are both sense-making objects. They are both experiencing entities.

I once had a discussion about spirituality where the other person said, But what if this world is all there is and there is no heaven or hell?

Well, that's part of the point. We've made all we need of heaven and hell right here in this existence.

Maybe this body, this one, mine, yours, this fleshly thing, this is the extent of eternity, is all there is of divinity; maybe there isn't anything else.

Maybe the mind doesn't understand. Maybe none of this thought matters. Matter matters. We are matter.

And as Fanny Howe wrote, *If this life isn't enough/ then an afterlife won't be enough.*

21 *Twenty-First Day*

LATE NIGHT

The guests have gone, the kitchen is clean.

We had eighteen people here tonight for fast-breaking meal.

I sat at one end of our long impromptu table, really three tables that fit together, and watched everyone talking with each other. I liked all the little groups, friends from various circles meeting each other.

Before the meal I asked everyone to reflect on all the various confluences of energy and individuals that brought the food to us and brought us together there.

In yoga it's called the "diamond net of Indra"—all the ways we are connected to each other through space and time. In Islam it is called kismet.

It is exciting to bring a community together at the end of the fast. One of the non-Muslim folks asked me what the physical part of the fast is like.

Unlike earlier in the month I am finding myself with greater energy now.

Now turning into the last week of fasting, both missing the fast in advance and also wondering what my life and body will feel like once I leave fasting behind.

Five of us went upstairs to the yoga and meditation room to pray. This was the second time in as many weeks that I have participated in communal prayer.

And for the first time in my own house.

I want to stay up longer, think more about all of this, but my first responsibility right now is to the practice of the fast. Which means I have to wake up in six hours, so now is the time for sleep.

22 *Twenty-Second Day*

LATE EVENING

Strictly speaking, after sunset this evening is the twenty-third of Ramadan and not the twenty-second.

I've always loved that a "day" in the Islamic calendar begins with the setting of the sun and continues through to the following sunset.

One begins not at midnight but at the ebb of light; in other words the ending of the daylight and not the morning is a more significant event.

I barely functioned today. Late in the month, exhausted by all the cooking and entertaining I did yesterday, I managed to rouse myself for a morning run and a meal, and then I did not sleep but stayed awake.

I went to a meeting at ten that lasted three hours, then I found myself at home with the whole afternoon and evening ahead of me. Unlike other days this month I found myself unable to be productive, or perhaps unwilling to be productive.

I remembered the fasting days of my childhood when we were encouraged to stay inside, watch TV or movies as ways of distracting ourselves, play games or otherwise occupy ourselves. I know now that the point of the fast is not to play diversionary tricks to distract oneself from the actual experience at hand, but at that time I only wanted to make it to the sunset so I could eat once more, and rejoin the so-called land of the living.

So today I indulged and watched not one but two movies.

The fast is starting to feel nearly ordinary now, ordinary in the sense of less difficult, but more importantly ordinary in the sense that every second, every minute isn't bringing delirious revelation. It's all just a little "ordinary."

Do I sound disappointed? I'm actually not. One of the problems I've had on my spiritual path is that I am always functioning in crisis. I can figure out my path at any given moment, but difficulty of circumstance always seems to be a theme.

I've haven't ever just been at a good place in my life and then practiced. Until now.

My home life, my professional life, my writing, my physical body practice—all of this now seems more or less manageable, even the difficult parts (my elbow is feeling much better today). So I'm in the third week of the fast with one week left to go. And it feels, well, ordinary. At last.

And thank god. I adore the chance to explore "ordinary."

Tonight of course is anything but ordinary. The twenty-third night of the month (in the traditional reckoning) is the actual night when the first verse of the Quran was revealed.

And of course the first word of the book was:

"Read."

"Read in the name of your Lord who created you."

"Created you from small clots."

Keeping in mind that medical science in sixth-century Arabia had not advanced yet to being able to describe the inner workings of the uterus and fallopian tubes, one notes that the Quran recognizes it is clots of tissue and not clay our actual bodies are made of.

The fast—restraint from food and water—
is a practice that helps us to know the body inti-
mately, most particularly through its limitations and weaknesses, though not always. Sometimes the body without food is actually a stronger body, sharper, keener, more in tune with the world around it.

And the body is like the year, the fasting month moving across it, shifting and changing throughout one's life time. The body is like the fasting month itself, with its own periods of activity and restraint, its own nights of revelation.

The body is like a day: it begins with the darkness of evening, ends with the ebbing of light.

Contains its own beginning nestled secretly inside.

3 *Twenty-Third Day*

LATE EVENING

A moth is flying around the lamp. I don't know how it got into the room since the windows are closed. Earlier in the summer we had fireflies in the room.

I'm irrationally afraid of bugs and insects, even (especially) butterflies, so I couldn't enjoy the fireflies' weirdly green incandescence.

I remember reading Satyajit Ray describing the end of his film *Aparajito*. Apu's mother comes to the door of her hut, looking out, presumably hoping to see Apu coming to see her in her illness.

She watches fireflies blinking in the forest. By this you are supposed to understand that she has died.

Of course Ray couldn't control the fireflies so he had actual crew members dressed in black with incandescent paper taped to their shirts running off into the woods.

I like a constructed art; art as artifice. Though I also love art completely unthought and spontaneous.

"Unthought" is of course untrue, because the very act of the artmaking is the product of countless deeds, actions, and thoughts that lead to that place.

In the second *Matrix* film, the Oracle offers Neo a candy. He asks her if she already knows whether he will take it or not. She says she does. The argument here is that though she is a machine she can well anticipate his choice based on all of his other past choices. You want to say that the human spirit has built-in anomalies, that we are utterly individual spirits, antithetical to prediction. You want to hope that's true.

Of course that very conundrum is the plot of the third film. There's a slight foreshadowing midway through the second film when Neo and Trinity make love in Zion, the last human city. You can see the plugs that run the length of Neo's spine. You realize then that he is part machine whether he chooses to be or not.

This is more or less the plot of much late twentieth-century and early twenty-first-century science fiction—the relationship between the individual human body and the machines that are coming to govern and direct our lives in ways benevolent and not quite: *The Matrix, The Terminator, Battlestar Galactica, Blade Runner, Freejack*, the list likely goes on.

Even in everyday reality, the regular body is fed by machines: farm machines, refrigerator trucks that drive vegetables thousands of miles, machines to build supermarkets, machines to package, process, and market foods, machines to engineer foods, machines to gas underripe foods to give them more color.

Unless you know the farmer who grew your food (or you grew the food yourself), unless you bought the fruits and vegetables, the dairy goods, and the meat from her or him, you too are fed by machines.

A firefly makes its own light, but a human is part of a vast network—a matrix if you like—of capitalist forces that provide him with energy, food, water, waste disposal, sustenance, information, and medical care.

We've moved so very far away from a local experience of our own bodies. When I practice yoga in the mornings, at the very least what I have is there and present; nothing is coming from far away; nothing (much) is outside myself.

When I see a firefly I do not think of death but I do think of a body that can make for itself what it needs, the way we are trying now to grow food in our backyard, and to buy all of our other vegetables from a local farm.

I want to come back to myself and know what I am made of.

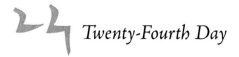 *Twenty-Fourth Day*

EARLY AFTERNOON

So I am sure there is something I've missed.

Well, many things I've missed. The month is almost over, I nearly got bored with the routine, and now I have this feeling that the month has slid by without me noticing.

But that's ridiculous, isn't it? I've been open to my experience the whole time, trying to write about the fast here, almost as it happens.

But that's not really true. I've kept my eyes open, but like a writer I've been processing and packaging the experience the whole time. Every time I sit down to write I only really have the vaguest ideas about where I want to go, but regardless the language leads me. I do arrive somewhere.

But on only a few of the days have I really just written random thoughts without trying to pull them together into some sense at the end.

Although I have focused very much on the body in the fasting process, my expression has been very intellectual and narrative, fractured though my paragraphs may be.

I've been running in the mornings, practicing yoga several times a week, experiencing this fast in my body. I've felt healthier and stronger, but I also hurt myself this month.

Despite the way I have very physically experienced the fast, and despite the fact that I mention from time to time that I am running or doing yoga, I haven't really talked in detail about my body's experience.

For example, I haven't explained that at the beginning of the month I was running three days on, one day off, distance-wise about three miles a day, until my knees protested a little bit, and I switched to running the same distance but every other day.

Nor that in my yoga practice I have been able now to lie down in *supta-virasana* for extended time periods and do not need to come up out of this position, nor that when I do, I have to move very tenderly from *virasana* to *sukhasana* to relieve the lower back.

I'm not sure my breath capacity has increased, but my ability to control it through the *surya-namaskar* has.

I was running about twenty-four miles a week before Ramadan started, and I am sorry that I had to cut back so dramatically, but I needed to.

Today, in my first yoga session after hurting my elbow,
I was very frustrated at not being able to do any arm
balances. I tried downward-facing dog, but even
that had a little twinge in it, so I just reasoned that
I would have to wait about two weeks before doing
more. Doris, my yoga partner, said: Yes, but Kazim,
two weeks is not really that long in a lifetime.

Twenty-nine days is not really that long in a lifetime
either.

The fasting month is heading to being over and I find
myself a little looking forward to that, but also a little
nostalgic.

But the fast returns. Another full month of fasts will
return in less than a year.

So ideally one hopes the benefits of fasting spread
past the month itself, spread into the full year that
follows.

Maybe next year I will try experiencing the fast
by mind, as well—reading scripture like I am
supposed to.

And perhaps letting the expression of the fasting
month be, rather than of the mind—essays—instead
of the body—poems—

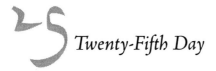 *Twenty-Fifth Day*

LATE NIGHT

My name, Kazim, means "patience."

Only it doesn't quite mean "patience" as much as it means a certain quality of "restraint."

A person with restraint is someone who is not overly affected by a series of bad events, also someone whose essential qualities are not really changed by a series of good fortunes either.

In other words, to me a Kazim is someone who might recognize his own essential and abiding nature as something that is beyond the momentary happenings of the immediate world, something beyond the fluctuations and agitations of the mind's consciousness.

A fasting Kazim might not be that different than a Kazim under any other circumstances.

I've always loved my name because while it is a very Shi'a name, it's not a very common Shi'a name.

The most famous Kazim in the world is an Iraqi pop star who, because he is Arabic-speaking (and not Urdu-speaking, like my family) spells his name differently: Kadem.

I've met a few other Kazims in my life but not very many. To my joy I met a Pakistani painter named Ali Kazim.

I have a cousin named Kazim.

Once a friend was visiting Pittsburgh and was standing in a line at a grocery store and overheard the women in front of him talking about a Kazim. The strange name in a strange place—he had to ask. And strangely, that turned out to be me these women were discussing.

The name Kazim as applied to me, though, is only an arrow, an icon like the ones on the altar upstairs, just an indicator for something I am reaching for.

My father was renamed because his mother thought she had not given him his true name properly.

A name is a gift to a person who exists beyond names.

Sometimes we rename ourselves.

"Kazim," or "I" if you prefer, does exist constantly though the mind must respond to all the things that happen around it. This is not a limitation but a human opportunity to actually know and understand the world.

By understanding the world I might just have a shot at understanding myself.

You might best know the name Kazim because the burial shrine of the man I was named after is in Baghdad, in a neighborhood called Kazimain.

The bridge to the shrine of Imam Musa al-Kazim collapsed on August 31, 2005, with hundreds of pilgrims on it. This may have been a result of poor crowd control.

At least the shrine still stands, unlike the Iraqi shrine of Imam Hasan Al-Askari, Imam Kazim's great-great-grandson, which was destroyed in successive bombings, first the dome in February 2006, and the two remaining minarets in June 2007.

Our names and the names of others around us are our own shrines to which we ought to make pilgrimage.

No bridge will collapse. No dome unravel.

We might find ourselves in the strangest of places.

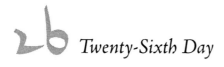 *Twenty-Sixth Day*

LATE EVENING

"Sometimes when you are fasting you feel very lonely," one of the speakers at the fast-breaking meal told a room full of Muslim and non-Muslim students.

It's true, but that was part of the charm for me. The fast was something secret inside, something I didn't have to share.

The Muslim Students Association had a wonderful idea: to invite campus community members to fast and to share the experience.

At the event we went around the room and students were invited to share their experiences of fasting.

One talked about how he realized how much of daily experience revolved around food, the getting of it, the eating of it. How to fill all that time?

Another talked of the experience as "approaching holiness."

Fasting is all these and more, I guess. The fast changes day to day throughout the month, and year to year for the constant practitioner.

To fast many times is like rereading a beloved book, but even fasting for only one day and only once will open some windows of perception for you.

The gathering was exciting because it was a participatory event—students were invited to share, and on each table there were markers to write on the paper tablecloths reflections of the day's experience.

Yes, I always considered my fast to be private, but perhaps reflecting on fasting so publicly this year in the online journal postings allowed me to share the practice with others in a community.

I know this is not unrelated to my new experiences with joining the communal prayer.

Today I joined them for the third time, and this time I didn't even think about it.

Somehow this month I stopped worrying about who would accept me or if I was "Muslim enough." I invited people into my home, I reflected on my own practice, I joined in the prayers.

Experiences start out extraordinary and then they become ordinary.

But what we pray for is that most special of gifts: to be able to see the ordinary as extraordinary once more.

Twenty-Seventh Day

Today was a strange day. So close to the end of the month of fasting, and I woke and did not eat balanced.

I ate rice pudding made from brown rice with a little soy milk, I had a fake-meat hot dog and I drank a cup of water and a cup of decaf coffee. Then I had some yogurt with berries. I knew I should be eating more fruits and vegetables to make sure I was getting my vitamins, but I was tired.

Not sleepy tired but tired of calculating everything, making sure I was eating enough of this or of that.

I went straight back to bed instead of staying up to write which is what I had normally been doing. I slept for four more hours then woke up and did an hour of yoga with one of my housemates.

After yoga I took to bed. Literally: I got my computer and a stack of books and a manuscript and I climbed into bed and for nearly five hours lay in bed and worked, sending emails, reading for a contest I am judging, and looking at my own poetry.

It wasn't really because I was fatigued, just tired. Tired of wandering around the day and not being able to have a cup of coffee, tired of not being able to meet people for lunch.

Tired of not being able to run in the daytime.

Every part of this month has been special and been a blessing, so this feeling at the end of the month must be a blessing as well.

I've—unexpectedly—not been looking forward to the end of fasting. I will miss the feeling of emptiness that foodlessness offers me. I will miss the weird focus that comes from removing consideration of this huge thing from my mental space.

After a day like today I will see that life, the life without fasting, is a blessing as well.

Does the fast, as the student yesterday said, help you to "approach holiness"?

But holiness is everywhere, in the ordinary days as well. Drinking water and eating food in the daytime as well. I want to spend all my secrets.

Will I ever share my secret fasting notebook?

28 *Twenty-Eighth Day*

LATE EVENING

Another day in bed. Granted, I was working the whole time. I had a pile of books, a manuscript, my laptop.

I finished an essay I'm writing on the work of Agha Shahid Ali, I wrote emails to contributors to a collection of essays on the work of Jean Valentine that I am editing. I worked a little bit on polishing a hybrid-genre prose manuscript I have been working on sporadically for about six years now.

The more I stayed in bed, the more I couldn't bear to get out, although today was a beautiful day, the sun was shining.

At a certain point I had to go and get groceries for our fast-breaking meal. There were nineteen people here tonight. There is some certain satisfaction in cleaning the kitchen fully after a big meal like that. I say that as someone who is not a "cleaner."

Still, I've picked up new habits this month that I haven't normally had, most all of them good ones.

So why have I so dramatically and quickly run out of steam in the last few days of the month?

Is this actually a secret boon, as I was explaining to some folks tonight?

There is no ascetic tradition in Islam, no monastic tradition, no celibate orders. One practices always as a layperson. You practice the pilgrimage and then you go home. You fast for a month and then the month is over.

The bare crescent of the moon will appear in the sky soon. The month will be over. Then I will return to my ordinary life and if I am lucky I will take some of the lessons of this month with me.

Today is also the first day of the Jewish new year. What a lovely hinge, reminding me of very recently when Ramadan started on Yom Kippur. We're being told in the most poetic (and ephemeral) way to sort ourselves out.

We have a chance today, as we did on September 12, 2001, to choose to see one another with empathy and love, to choose understanding.

My body is a boat on the ocean of endlessness. In the Quran, the storm lasted forty days and forty nights.

And then the bird came with tidings in its mouth.

Well, I think we are each other's bird now. If peace seems a long way off that is only because peace is actually right in front of us, but we haven't yet opened our mouths to take the leaf in our teeth.

We owe each other home.

29 *Twenty-Ninth Day*

LATE MORNING

Last night I was combing through websites trying to figure out if yesterday or today would be the last day of fasting.

Though it is still very traditional to observe the fast until the barest line of the first quarter moon shows itself, there are many who say one can consult and follow the more precise astronomical knowledge of the present day.

My heart leapt when I found a website telling me that the eighteenth of the month would be the last day of fasting—yesterday.

But another authority said the fast always lasts through the twenty-ninth day, and if the moon is not seen that evening, then fasting would continue for a thirtieth day.

I thought to myself, after an hour or more of cleaning in the kitchen, that I might skip today's fast. After all, I told myself, I had fasted twenty-eight straight days, a full month. I'd "had" "the experience." Right?

A decision to skip the last day of fasting might have been easier if I'd had a stronger last two days. But I'd been in bed the whole time, mentally active, but barely moving. It didn't feel real to me. *I* didn't feel real to me.

(Though it occurs to me now: What if the entire month of fasting is to bring you to that place exactly— too weakened in both body and spirit to stand up, lying in bed, an unmoving entity, yet still aware, still perceiving. Another answer to the question "Who am I?")

One fasts during the fasting month because one is enjoined so to do. But what if I chose it. At the close of the month, whether one "had to" or not, what if this were mine—my day of fasting, a fast because I wanted it.

The month had been a container, a vessel to pour myself into, a vessel that would hold the formlessness of the self in the form of the ritual.

Maybe part of the point is this: To go on when there is no desire to go on. To practice when practice is burdensome.

Even that is easy, in the framework of the month of fasting. You hit a hump and you work through or go around. But what if that ritualized support isn't there? Is this the last day of fasting or was it really yesterday, in which case this day's fast is unnecessary?

Not unnecessary, because I choose today's fast myself. I savor each moment.

There are those who fast during the year also; I've never managed the willpower to be one of them. Which is why I so much look forward to Ramadan each year because then fasting is a choice that is made for me, the way a mother would choose for you.

If my fasts this month have been working within the network of a community, however peripherally, my fast today is entirely personal, between me and One-That-Is.

The moon is somewhere unseen in the sky. The stars were so bright this morning as I ran, shining from millenia ago to remind me.

Of the passing of things.

Some things are set up for you. A month in which you fast. The rules you follow to fulfill them.

But other things you have to understand inside your own body and heart. How the fast affects you. What the fast is for. What and how the fast teaches you.

As I chose the fast this day, for myself, I know that the world and god, whatever god is, is both everywhere around me but also everywhere within me.

Just like the prophet Mohammed's face and Gabriel's face are blanks in classical paintings of them showing the exchange of Quranic verses, what I learned this month is a blank. I see the outlines, but not what it actually is, because it is experiential. I learned it by doing, and though I've tried explaining, the larger part is the experience itself, the way you cannot really learn about climbing a wall or running in the dark or a particular yoga posture until you've climbed or run or twisted.

Moses' revelations were written in fire on stone. Mohammed's revelations were whispered into his ear in the dark of the cave. One of these men had to read and then write. The other had to listen and then recite.

I don't care about the astronomical calculation of the moon, that ability which existed even in the sixth century CE. And I don't care to check a website or wait by the phone to hear from someone else whether a *maulana* in Toronto or Qum or some other place has seen the moon and declared the month over.

I will go out tomorrow and look for the moon and see for myself.

Absence of Stars:
A Fasting Journal

For my mother

First Day

To empty myself in the afternoon.

White sunlight comes through the window.

I walk through the apartment trying to reposition
the plants to catch the most light, elephant-ears
velvet green, a drop of dew at the tip of each leaf.

The jade petals become white and thick and the
branches spread in the sunlight.

I put five petals in a bowl and wrapped it in a page
of poetry.

To leave him something of mine.

He placed a carved wooden Buddha in a bowl and
stitched a wrapping of mulberry leaves around it.

We decide we will open these gifts when we once
again share a house.

Between that time and now, the space of silence, the
empty bowl, the speechlessness of the figure or the
poetry, the passing to dust of the mulberry leaves
acting as the surface of his gift and the jade petals
inside my gift, wrapped in a page of poetry.

The green surface and wood core of his gift inverse to the paper surface and green core of my gift.

I emptied myself out into the bowl of a diffuse afternoon, leaves of text scattering into the late summer, yellow paper trickling into the ground.

Will I find my way back to myself I briefly wondered.

I'd already let the feeling pass and was looking in a different direction.

The plants are all outdoor plants, not meant to grow inside.

Second Day

When I walked in the garden, late September, the lotuses already past, their withered seedpods thrusting up, bare of petals.

Green on the surface of the water.

Alone in the park and hungry. Hungry and irrelevant.

Irrelevant because unable to act.

Time was I woke without an alarm and slept with ease at night.

Now I have to struggle to rise in the dark, to feed myself, to prepare myself for a long day without food, a boat carved hollow so it can float on the surface of the sea.

The space in the room of the wind created only by time.

This rug, six feet by nine feet, silk, lush and thick, but so fine it folds into eighths and fits into the car trunk. I put it down in each apartment I move into.

The road of time.

Days I am hungry I stretch myself into the air and want to be empty, want to empty myself into the air.

The way water comes from a faucet into a cup or water passed from cup to cup I want to pass or be passed.

Cups of white septemberlight, summer that yawns and stretches thin, reaching into autumn.

3 *Third Day*

The hunger is something you dig a hole in yourself to bury.

Earliest morning, the first part of the self, is the bleakest and emptiest place.

Absence inside absence, you walk the streets.

What is cleaner than fire, more brilliant than the awareness of how large the moon is, how heart-breaking that people have been there.

The hunger inside you, hold it.

Every time you pass someone or speak to them you know you have it.

Your body knows it is alive, you do not forget.

Give the elephant-ears a half-turn in the window. They twist toward the light.

What do you turn toward.

A book of winds, on the white light of a cloudy late afternoon.

When you haven't drunk any water you sag a little bit too, can't remember where you're going, even try to write less to save the ink in your pen.

Because when will you get another.

Body or pen.

The feeling inside is not of emptiness but a peculiar fullness of lack.

The feeling is yours and even at the end of the day, a cup of water at your lips, you find yourself wanting to hold onto it.

Fasting is first to abstain and then to embrace emptiness.

Then to give emptiness back.

Fourth Day

You're tired after eating and there's no time for you,
your own mind.

Instead you're tidying or looking for paperwork.

Marco stitched all the mulberry leaves together.

In Kaaterskill Falls in the winter the thin waterfall
freezes into a pillar of ice.

The mind does wander.

Full after a day of fasting you feel wrapped up in the
solidity of air.

Hungry during the day as if you are a bowl, bone dry,
or a leafless tree the wind blows through.

Soon friends are visiting, you have to give a talk.

But you would give anything to lie down.

You want to exercise, but after twelve hours of hunger
how will you lift yourself.

You're not even there, but if it is not you that's there
then who's there.

Saturday you shared the fence with a small, black, long-
haired spider.

He crawled onto your wrist and when you saw him
there you shook him off, but by instinct not fear.

You crouched down to look at him, his lovely eyes,
funny expression looking back at you.

For a while after that you kept feeling him on your
skin.

Even now in the empty apartment you imagine
him hiding in some secret place. As if somewhere
unseen in the big apartment there's a small soul that
is looking at you.

5 Fifth Day

In the mornings I leave early to run around the
square before I eat.

Because I want my body to feel its motion, its blood,
to be alive in the long hallway of morning.

My body a flame in the air combusting.

These are drugs I take.

Tomorrow after twelve hours of fasting I am meet-
ing the son of a friend who is going to teach me
how to climb at the climbing wall.

Strange to be inside climbing up a fake wall though
I have no desire to climb in the wild.

Also to be a student again.

To be strong in the well of weakness I do this.

I've woken alone, eaten alone, been alone through-
out most of the day, hungering and alone.

Today I went to a meeting of Muslim students but
it was strange for me, to be among others.

I like the solitude of the fast.

A book I wrote in which I tried to say something true has been accepted for publication. But I am afraid.

You can't always be alone.

You do sometimes have to speak.

At the end of fasting, one is required to break the fast.

The purity of hunger, no matter how cleansing, in a fast is required to be temporary.

Though it frightens you almost to death you have to tell about your life.

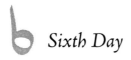 *Sixth Day*

At the beginning of the day you rise in darkness, not what you're used to.

Living death to go from sleep to dark bed into darkness still, no sunlight on the horizon or even blue twilight.

There is no light like the rich thickness of blue before sunrise; if you have not seen it then you have not seen it.

You minister yourself slowly task by task. From a dream of a life you make a life.

Last night I went to a meeting of Muslim students and felt uncomfortable.

Who was I but a stranger.

In the morning after you've had a last glass of water to "seal the fast" the day pulls itself taut from your fingers, is a string stretching away from you to the sunset.

A string you could pluck.

A string and it is yours.

The day is an empty bowl you hold in your hands.

Reading the spare verses, touching your body now and again during the day to remind yourself your physical existence is real, your body is alive, despite the dissipation of your mind into clouds and space, there really is a world.

Last afternoon in front of the sink just the mere task of washing dishes becomes significant dish by dish.

I held the big orange salad bowl Mom bought me along with four small orange bowls in 1998 when I was offered a job teaching at the local community college.

But instead of taking the job, I went to New York and I haven't lived at home since.

My mother, my love, wanted me to come home. Orange salad bowl set to tell me.

Growing up I always knew my mother would fast with me. Something the two of us shared in the house. Neither my father nor my sisters fasted in those days.

So my mother and I hungered together each year for a month, grew thin together, wondered together.

There was a world in which we loved each other that no one else lived in.

Seventh Day

Sounds like a desert.

Each minute a slow and solid object.

In the time of hunger I try to find friends to talk to, something to distract me—chores, television, reading poems for class, anything not to be alone with emptiness and time.

What is the fast? Preparation for death? For spiritual deprivation?

To know the body is mortal, connected by essential materials to the substance of the earth.

To know we are not unique from creation, as if humans developed a sense of superiority the minute angels loved Adam, who understood.

8 *Eighth Day*

This evening I cooked rice squares, wrapped them in a cloth napkin to take with me to the climbing wall.

The fire alarm kept going off; I had to wave a towel in front of it.

Afternoon, hours, evening: Walking through the square; fire truck sirens.

Wondering if it was my house on fire.

I dreamed my house was on fire. How can you even tell about it.

The body is not starving. The body actually grows long without food. Looking down the tracks toward the end of its life, meaning the earth in a fast no longer curves.

Poring over a chair to see how it is made, the body is that much of a physical object.

The universe notwithstanding.

What does light lose passing through a window.

More appropriately can you measure the minute portion of what is left behind.

The dream of fasting: me holding something against my chest—an empty bowl.

I never dreamed of lack as central to existence until I learned about the eye of a hurricane. And felt them pass over me when the hurricanes hit New York City in 1979.

No one told me how to live.

Every night at the end of a fast my mother and I would sit down to a small dish of dates and two cups of warm water.

Mother Teresa doubted. Which makes her more, not less, holy.

I do not drink at the end of a fast because I am thirsty but because I am making a choice to leave paradise and return to the earth.

9 *Ninth Day*

The elephant-ears did not do well when I left for a weekend without watering them.

Now with water and a space by the window the plant is recovering but it has been many days since I've seen the little drop of water on the leaf-tip as before.

The morning is like vapor. Various tasks and chores during the day, so this is the moment I can pause in time.

My mind always goes back to the Shadyside house, to the comfort of returning from a day of work at the office, going for a run in the country, returning home to sit on the deck, drunk on the afternoon, drinking green tea and eating toast and honey, watching the sunset.

That was exactly when and where I came into poetry and reached toward my future life.

Loneliness as hard as the bones under my skin.

Silence in the night—crickets and afterthoughts.

Each morning I am up early enough to look at the moon, now waning, and the morning star.

There is no name for the thick crepuscular blue.

How solid and tactile a sky can appear.

My book of sentences, the story of my life, now at the threshold.

A friend says I should wait to publish it.

These are sentences I barely pronounced.

If you see truly through a fast, feel you have stripped some essential thing between you and the world away, is it possible then that you are also as seen, as bare to other people around you.

10 *Tenth Day*

At the end of the day aren't you a prisoner not to the liberation but to the wish that this current hunger would end.

You could stay here forever in want.

On Saturday the police roughed up a student who questioned them about an arrest.

Canceling appointments to go to a meeting about the affair.

Things in the world—whether it is temporary or mere illusion—are real: Things really do happen.

It's not raining but my skin feels it is raining.

Marco is arriving tomorrow night; every night in bed my skin misses his.

We fast from the presence of one another.

Our awareness of absence is active.

I've misunderstood and understood in the same moment which is how I know that all of this, the fast, my thinking about it, is part of the same practice.

Mosques I won't go inside, people I won't speak to.

Meeting my friend's son to go to the climbing wall,
but going home because he wasn't there.

Hearing about my nephew's difficulties in school and
remembering my own.

Species of the queerest sort of shame: Shame that
your body is not correct, does not belong in the world.

⅄⅄ Eleventh Day

The fast is to restrain.

For so long I believed my name to mean "patience"
until someone told me it meant "restraint," which
does not feel the same.

In one, an abiding quality, passive and innate; in the
other, a form of negating action.

Not enough to fast from food and water—one is also
asked to refrain from loud talking, coarse language,
gossip, anger, smoking, smelling tempting food,
immersion of the head in water, sexual intercourse.

How can I choose from the list and after the sun goes
down which of these practices is allowed back in.

Outside the window the light is orange.

Unlike in New York I have begun to sleep through
the night.

In fasting you are supposed to forget yourself and
remember creation, a promise that binds you.

The exchange, if one willfully breaks a fast for which
one has made ritual intention: To buy the freedom of
sixty slaves.

Always something missing, only what I've wanted to pour into you.

So I empty myself not to be filled but to experience the emptiness.

I leave the world to observe my appetite for it.

12 *Twelfth Night*

A repeating line from Surah Rahman: "Which then of the bounties of your Lord would you deny?"

It's a challenge, *refusal* being the sin here. The world is not mere testing ground but garden.

We were not perhaps cast out from anywhere but rather given a gift, this mortal world, a world that can live and can die.

To die means to come back through this moment.

In some philosophies, Creator and Creation not separate.

Late now, past midnight and I should be sleeping to wake early but instead distract myself, by reading, watching a movie, staying up.

The stove needs to be fixed, the bathroom recaulked.

Yesterday I left the house after cooking, worried the smoke alarms would again go off.

I'm alone here and if something happened to me no one would be here to save me.

When Marco had surgery this summer he was so vulnerable and weak I had to take care of him.

His body was frail, his eyes half-lidded, crusted black-red blood around his nostrils.

Every day I would prepare our meals, clean the dishes, working on thinking of no one but him.

Absent-mindedly, I had closed the bathroom door which he then crashed into, banging his nose, cursing in the night.

Fragile house, my little body, a body that is mine but is not mine.

Says Desikachar, "The world exists to be lived in and experienced." And then later, "The world exists to set you free."

13 Thirteenth Day

You cannot move as fast as you want, run from one thing to another. Everything has become immaterial and longer.

This morning, the boys who live in the apartment downstairs were shouting. I don't say anything about it because their mother is there alone with them.

To be here alone.

I've learned how to do it. Partly I like having an open space of time.

Fasting was a secret between my mother and me. We held hands invisibly throughout the day.

A fast between people holds each of them to what's between, to that which goes beyond the corporeal connection.

It's always easier to fast with another person. We feed each other our hunger.

Her hand had been my pillow.

My mother, love of my life. Every time I leave her presence is a fast from her.

Active attention to lack.

As I leave, she holds a Quran over my head. By traveling under it we hope to return safe to each other.

Journeying from the beginning—darkness—to the end—darkness—of a day. Of a life.

14 *Fourteenth Day*

A student was assaulted by the town police, so there is a meeting of the community and we try to get information, which reminds me of back in Shippensburg when for a critical afternoon my body did not belong to me.

Was seen instead as an instrument and locus for violence.

A threat.

This body, the one getting thinner and thinner, engendering its ultimate refusal to aggression.

To make the brooding words of death disappear.

Holding the breath in, retention of energy.

Holding the breath out, retention of restraint.

I remember these concepts from yoga practice, but the Islamic practice of fasting has taught me this *inside* the internal body.

These two forces, energy and restraint, travel the double helix, the pathways of the brain, the red and blue roads of blood, like the traveling of water from the ground into the plants into the air and back.

In every way I return to you.

I hold myself back in the fast so I can return to you.

Fasting, pilgrimage, prayers, forms of returning
to you.

We want our voices to be heard not only in eternity
but in this world. When I speak now, I hear the low
tones and spareness of my own speech.

The students are being excluded from the
discussion.

Flustered and afraid for their safety they do not
want to be spoken for, but to speak.

15 *Fifteenth Day*

I gave a reading this afternoon, read poems and talked about my sources.

I was there and not there, loved the feeling of being loved and also can barely remember.

Images—the ocean floor, the horizon—led me from book to book, across years and time.

Noticing for the first time how the architecture of sound changed, the line and the sentence.

When I was asked questions—about the difference between poetry and prose, my love of music, the role of sound in poetry, I seemed to answer not personally, not about myself, but broadly, even politically.

Aftermath of exposure is cloak.

Also for the first time ever I read from my autobiography of sentences.

The lonely threads that enabled me to speak, because I would speak in sentences not paragraphs.

Literally without consequence.

From the threads a picture emerged; I found I had to explain nothing.

Pure speech bracketed by time, and by writing all this down I lived.

Here in the airport, the empty airport, I wait for Marco to arrive from Newark.

And to end my fast from him.

My joyful life, his arrival.

 *Sixteenth Day*

A hot day today: In the late afternoon three hours
before fast-breaking we are like plants listing to
one side.

Irritation, tenderness, devotion and distraction are all
somehow happening at once.

A band carols through the street and we are going
from drums to drums, a Taiko performance happen-
ing in the field.

To surround yourself with music, one note by one
note.

Downstairs one of the boys strumming noisily on a
guitar.

Music goes quickly from one moment to another
sometimes holding both history and possibility in its
articulations.

Also, the transition as a violinist bows across strings
or a drummer raises and lowers his hands between
energy and restraint.

A constant exchange, as in the infinity symbol and the
zero symbol I saw tattooed on the man's shoulders in
a yoga class.

Amounting to the same number, especially when tattooed on an individual's skin, the body being the opposite of both zero and infinity.

When does afternoon turn to evening.

How, Marco wants to know, did early Muslims know the times of the call to prayer.

When so accurately by satellite and website rather than the imprecision of human eye and voice are these mapped today.

Ways you know the fast is over:

> a newspaper
>
> the palm of a hand held out
>
> a white thread and a black thread
> hung in the window
>
> the hairs on your forearm
>
> the moon visible in the sky

When the threads are indiscernible from one another. When you cannot see the hairs on your arm. When you can no longer see the fortune-lines.

There is an instant of a moment and you cannot know.

Seventeenth Day

At the beginning of the day.

The cicadas have not yet struck up their sound so everything is shocking and quiet.

In the silence of the beginning one does not eat for flavor but for sustenance. The subtler tastes like a sour apple or a carrot or sliced tomatoes feel as sweet as needed.

Some mornings I eat oatmeal, nuts, toast and peanut butter, all foods that bring me through the day.

Today: a bowl of fiber cereal, soy milk, a small ginger gold apple, a plate of tomatoes with kosher salt.

To eat is a gift. Hunger points you to it.

To restrain—with intent—from eating is also a gift and points you to a greater understanding of all kinds of inequity, not just political.

We have enough to feed everyone.

We know how to reduce the greenhouse emissions.

We only have to stop using creatures for food and stop equating food with money.

When one is in a fast, in the early afternoon, as one walks slowly through the apartment turning plants halfway in their pots, all this seems very easy.

It is eight in the morning. The light is pure.

Marco cannot fast since he is supposed to be taking medicine. The fast is once again only mine.

I am in front of eleven hours of fast but feel for the moment as full as I ever have.

18 *Eighteenth Day*

The month starts not in the pure absence of the new moon but in the sighting of the very first sliver of the waxing moon.

As in possibility we begin.

This month the full moon was very low, near the horizon, night's sunflower.

One night managing to burn its light through very thick coal-black clouds, billowing apart from it as from a fire.

Moon light is actual sunlight, one must be reminded.

Only reflected.

A body is like that also, a moon in space reflecting all of consciousness.

Reflecting everything that came before and predicting everything that will come after, local in an eternal constant.

You can see this if you stop for a moment your body's motions.

Internal motions stopped in the fast.

Sometimes in the morning after eating I want to go back to bed and lie down, I want to distract myself by reading or make time go quicker by watching television or surfing the Internet.

But I ought to be alone with myself in the natural world.

Alone used to mean without other people but now I feel that alone means without all the extensions— computers, phones, televisions.

To fast means to fast from all of this too, perhaps.

19 *Nineteenth Day*

Lucille Clifton asks, *have we not been good children/ did we not inherit the earth?*

At my weakest, in the late afternoon during a visit to the zoo, walking here and there to see the animals.

A moment to think but stretch myself between dark and dark. Time takes the place of the body.

Marco, upset by the zoo, sensitive to the animals in captivity, existing only for our sight.

And in giving oneself to time, to hours between now and the moment I next take food and water, the only way to do it is to vanish from an awareness of time into the exact individual moment.

Not "Eternity in an hour" as Blake said, but merely "Eternity in."

Body's weariness translates itself to slow movements, slackening awareness.

You don't think of three things at once as you normally would, but instead really focus on watering plants, doing the dishes.

Can't touch anything. Can't own anything.

Even speaking to someone new, talking about yourself, receiving information in the ears, learning how to answer, all requires energy, actual caloric energy.

The scene outside: A tree, vines climbing up and sheathing the trunk, leaves, limpid, limp, yellow and white.

Give the plant another half-turn toward the sun.

In the last part of the day *now* can slow down immensely to the feeling of water evaporating into the air.

Feelings might condense.

But the passage between the ground and the air is the body of a person who fasts.

20 *Twentieth Day*

Always the feeling of waiting for something.

Sometimes harder with another person who is not fasting since we always end up talking about food.

How the world was taken and cultivated for food, minerals, and energy; not as sustenance for every being but as riches for those who could hold on to them.

There must be a relationship between that and this, the willful withholding from food.

Inherent peacefulness and support between two people who are sharing the fast, or is it not that at all, but rather purely individual and internal.

A change in attitude that is fundamental.

By fasting you isolate your individual body from the network of food and luxury and energy distribution, the unsustainable consumption, the combustion of matter into energy on not only a planetary but cosmic scale, rather than a system that preserves, maintains, and nurtures—earth, air, and water balancing themselves.

The fire of the individual is not in service of that balance but in service of ego, desire, derangement, danger.

It's really only to live that my mother and I used to sit down to a plate of dates and cups of warm water at the end of each evening.

You deny the body fresh and filling food so you can feel clean, so you can know the purity of hunger, know what the building of the body is in its actual state unaffected by the energy of the external sources.

Love is in the flesh and walls of the body, the chambers and spaces, the backroads and highways, which lead from place to place, connecting each system to the others.

Mother, you've taught me about the body which is to say about sunset, about time and entropy, about death and the planet, about breath and the space-less universe.

21 *Twenty-First Day*

The elephant-ears begin to now grow toward the sun, though without the jewel of dew at the leaf-tips I used to see.

The horizontal cradle of the waning moon hovered this morning in a triangle of bright lights, one of which must have been Venus.

I'll look at a star-chart later to see.

We go quietly from room to room.

Yellow leaves are trickling down from the walnut tree, a slow rain.

A mulberry tree next to the walnut tree; because of Yoko Ono's song a mulberry tree will always mean to me the beginning of voice after the voicelessness of starvation.

We hold fast to a commitment to peace in the midst of years of war; holding fast means skin to skin and not releasing.

To fast in the face of violence is to make yourself most vulnerable; to refuse to feed oneself is to be an infant again, to be again at the mercy of a reality you decline to control.

To make everyone around a parent to you.

They will provide and feed.

Fortunate to have the fasting month in the beginning of autumn.

As we let go of our bodies and ask that our appetites not be too determinant of our lives or our spiritual direction, we are lucky to be in autumn, and so this action is paralleled by the earth itself preparing to fast.

We learn at the beginning of our fast, in the early hours, what it feels like to release the leaves and prepare for winter.

22 Twenty-Second Day

Because of Islam's lunar calendar, based on a lunar year, which is eleven days shorter than the solar year, the fasting month will move backward through the seasons during my life.

When I was living at home, about ten years ago when Mom and I fasted together, the fast was in the middle of the winter and we would break our fast at sundown around four-thirty in the afternoon.

Though the day was shorter, somehow the fast seemed no easier.

This was the season of a heartbreak for me and at the time I was willing to try anything to live.

I've never managed a regular practice of the daily prayers in all my years of fasting.

Some people have discounted my practice of fasting since this is only the second pillar of faith.

Why practice the second pillar of faith while ignoring the first, prayer, perhaps thus more essential, they ask.

Especially considering that the fast, the second pillar and supposedly "lesser" practice, is so physically rigorous, life-consuming—whereas the more primal practice of prayer is so simple, so easy to integrate into daily life.

Odd to have been outside in the dark pre-dawn, to know what the world looks like, hidden, occulted, and to see it now, in the gold-yellow morning light.

Why fast—active restraint—without prayer—passive declaration.

No one can talk to breath or spirit but ask to answer or answer to ask.

Sound of Marco drinking and swallowing tea.

By fasting we work to quiet all the active engagements of the body and environment: To try to actually see what is happening.

We pray best by opening ourselves like a book.

We will then be written in or perhaps moreso be written.

23 *Twenty-Third Day*

In the afternoon.

We spent the morning in chores, washing dishes, tidying up the table. Put up curtain rods and curtains: the cream off-white ones I got when I lived in Rhinebeck.

I was so proud of them when I bought them, translucent shady light coming through them, the yellow-gold afternoon light filtered to white.

We cleaned the screens of each window, dusted in every corner we could reach.

After washing the curtains I hung them outside to dry.

To spend a Sunday in the house doing these ordinary things.

In this empty month I find myself strangely turning.

From an external life, you would think, to an internal one, but really in both directions at once.

24 Twenty-Fourth Day

I've not found agency or voice to write very much about the world and the people around me, especially the person I love.

For many years a self-imposed silence.

Recently I've written and written to get myself through this.

In a book called *Bright Felon* I try to explain how we delineate human acts as crimes.

To talk of Islam at all is to talk of changing the direction of worship—from the Far Mosque, thought to be the actual route to Heaven, a metaphor perhaps for the internal life, to the Near Mosque, what is close by, that which is within and among humans and animals.

The fast takes us from a self-oriented universe into creation.

How you can notice the light, the elephant-ears, the alarming sound of walnut fruit hitting the earth.

Rather than worry about the pronunciation of prayers or even the direction in which to send them, actually look at a person's face, listen to a person's voice.

25 *Twenty-Fifth Day*

Voices heard through the screen door.

Last night the muted gong of the gamelan ensemble.

Years ago before I had seen a gamelan I had an idea
in my imagination of what a single instrument
played by many people would look like.

Not imagining the gamelan in little pieces, but as
a room-sized whole, each musician with her own
station, cymbal or string—

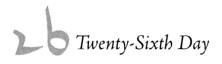 *Twenty-Sixth Day*

Reading now Eboo Patel's book about the necessity of connecting political action with community service.

This is if the individual body can be seen as a community of human interests.

We all speak about poetry, the eternally deep night sky, the way we ought to be talking about the human body, about the actual dirt of the earth, the ways it is used, moved, appropriated.

I'm in the last stages of the fast, mid to late afternoon, two and a half hours to sunset.

Odd to choose to come back to the journal, now at one of my five appointed times for prayer.

To look into the night sky is to see into the beginningless beginning of force and time.

I've not yet said the most quotidian parts—what I eat for breakfast each morning, an hour-by-hour chronicle of physical sensation associated with a fast, how it feels later in the evening after having eaten.

The feelings are broad and slow. You cannot simply say, "I am hungry," because it's not really "hungry" that you are.

I remember food but not what it is to eat.

My body is a transitional site, a holding pattern.

I dream to come back, to have it be really mine
again, my lovely brother, my *corps*, my shield.

Twenty-Seventh Day

To see the inside, one's own body, using the outside—
one's self as an individual in the world.

What does all this have to do with the fast.

More importantly, why am I, feeling separated from
the *ummah* as a group, declining to participate in either
communal or individual prayers, choosing now to
return to the fast, accepting fasting as a practice.

In a sense my old teacher Jonji sent me back to fasting
when he returned to teaching in the wake of discover-
ing his cancer.

After he understood his limited time forward—I imag-
ined the experience was like walking down a hallway,
seeing the end, the painting of two fish hanging there,
knowing you were coming to it.

The end of a fast a version of that.

Being always Muslim, but also *through* and outside it,
before and after it, all at once.

To fast for justice, to dream past our own obsession
with death, not passing through the fear but escaping it.

I'm looking out the window at the gray darkening,
the onslaught of evening: Sunset at this moment.

For a moment whether I eat or drink doesn't matter.

For a moment I don't drink, not because I am not
thirsty but because my present state is of abstinence
and it merely continues itself.

I have neither desire to eat and drink nor desire to
continue the fast.

The way a body seeks to breathe and live.

And when I do take a sip of the water it is not to
slake thirst but only because evening has now fully
fallen and now is the prescribed time to break
the fast.

8 *Twenty-Eighth Day*

Night, and Marco has returned to New York.

The oldest leaf on the plant is turning from a deep brilliant green, fading to white.

It took me a very long time—years and years really—to think I could speak about anything.

Only last year Rachel Tzvia Back explained to me that unlike Ishmael, Isaac did not know what his father intended in the thicket.

There was a son who felt betrayal and shock at what his father had intended for him.

My father and I are still trying to find our way to each other, sure of nothing but love.

In the mornings I wake up to run: I run because I believe in the beauty of the body and what the world is like when we move consciously through it.

I fast because one cannot be excluded, as one could be excluded from communal prayer or pilgrimage: Fasting is the quietest act and needs no other to participant to make it real.

Unlike prayer, which is a cognitive exercise within a physical framework, fasting unites the body and the mind in a single practice.

The fast is a contract between the spirit and the creator, between a single body and all the material of creation.

The contract binds these four, one to the other and the road they travel: Energy and restraint.

To run or dance is one part, the fast and the breaking of the fast another.

A month of fasting means you see day after day through an entire heavenly cycle short enough for one to experience this as a single "moment" but long enough to feel it sink in.

And rigorous enough a practice that fasting literally changes your body's physical makeup.

You give some matter back to creation as energy.

29 Twenty-Ninth Day

As the month goes to its last week I grow distant.

There was a school shooting in Cleveland. A fourteen-year-old boy shot five people non-fatally and then killed himself.

I found myself glad and saying it was good that no one was killed, forgetting that someone was.

Or did he forfeit my concern by acting with such extreme violence against others.

How do you reconcile a position against violence with compassion for those who commit it.

I know people who have killed: A friend, gentle and humorous, was in the infantry in Iraq; he talks a lot about the war, even about opposing it, but does not talk about whether he killed anyone.

Fasts that break.

To break a tradition or a heart or the truth.

To break the truth is to tell it.

To break a fast is to seal it: By eating again you put

the abstinence in past tense and thus make it real, a
positive attribute, not mere lack or absence.

Returning the body to its material boundaries,
not an entity but an eternity of phenomena, an
exchange of matter in which one must participate.

3⁰ Thirtieth Day

In his sermon today, Brother Ali said that we fast to remind ourselves that on an everyday basis there is something we are missing—we are separated from our spiritual source.

Too many people still view bodily death as the end, and spiritual death as irreversible, when we are all fasting creatures, at every moment appearing and disappearing in original hunger.

To not eat, because we are not content merely to eat.

When we engage in fasting, this is a manageable practice of that kind of equanimity that will not choose between life and death.

In Shi'a Islam the five pillars of faith are beliefs: oneness of divinity, justice of divinity, a belief in messengers and messages, presence of a teaching lineage, and a belief that there will be an accounting for our lives and deeds.

In Sunni Islam the five pillars of faith are practices: prayers, fasting, poor tax, charity, and pilgrimage.

Taken together they offer a beautiful picture. As I listened to the sermon I wondered what kind of Muslim I was.

I know I am a Muslim; the month of fasting spoke that to me even if I weren't listening, but still I felt alone in the room, unsure what I shared with these men, unable to reconcile my own beliefs with what was being preached.

The service seemed very superficial, unimportant—people were talking during the *qutba*, arriving late, leaving early.

I would find it hard to describe how this community shaped my understanding of being a Muslim.

How all my deeply held spiritual beliefs collided with my awakening to love and the nature of my body, my heart.

It is a heartbreaking question: Am I, by my life, excluded from the *ummah*.

The active practices of community—pilgrimage, prayer, authority of the teaching lineage—hold no substantive interest for me as they relate to the intensity of my faith.

"The rose is my *qibla*, the wind is my black stone," wrote the poet Sohrab Sepehri, and I hold fast to practices where the individual walks a lonely road, where exclusion has no meaning, where one is alone with God.

"You have the wrong idea about Islam," my uncle once admonished me, "if you think anyone can exclude you."

I do feel I've hardly started anything—hardly become the writer I'm supposed to be, hardly yet loved my partner and my family the way I can, hardly learned yet about the nature of the world and all we can do here and what my part will be.

All of these, the war, the end of time, the incredible rage of history, the planet itself unraveling—we are not meant in these times to merely live; to do so would be as close as anything could be to sin.

Eden is over, if ever Eden was real.

I fast as the very beginning of an awareness of the disappearing and dissolving world.

Coda:
Breaking the Fast

At some point in the late afternoon, you come to a terrifying point in the fast—when you confront the blankness of the day.

Hours and hours remain and what do you say to that silence?

Or you come to the end of fasting, the end of the day or the end of the month and what have you learned, what have you said, have you come any closer to understanding?

Each minute that passes is harder, takes you farther and farther from having learned anything.

Where is your home, who are you, what is the condition of your body, for what purpose do you give yourself to practice?

To live as a body in a world of matter means you are part of the matter, participating in it in some way; or are you mere conduit, a passage of flesh through which matter and energy are converted to one another?

Yogi, Muslim, artist, teacher, lover of all creatures, you fast and draw the light in, hold it there, push the light out, hold your body in emptiness and space.

The month of fasting is over but I want to continue. How soon before I return here?

And how do I continue past the fasting month the connection that fasting offers?

During the last four days of fasting I found myself unable to write but also not actually experiencing the sensations of the fast the way I did in previous weeks.

I was at a poetry reading in which two poets, who had collaborated on a book, read from the book together, starting and finishing one another's sentences.

Contrary to the half-recited lines in their reading, they did not write the book back-and-forth between them but worked very hard to create a unified third voice.

Who is that third voice, a voice between two people, neither one nor the other, neither embodied nor disembodied?

I'm fastening myself to community awareness but a community in which I can have an actual role, actual personhood.

Now the month is over and we are supposed to get

ready for colder months and then the very long winter.

Pulling the fast through the fasting month and along with me. To begin with it as a quality, to find a place for it in my continuing life.

Not agreeing on Ramadan's start date and stop date is part of that fluidity. They could be at any time really.

Marco really wants to know: What else is like that—months starting on different days a couple of towns apart, based on local cloud conditions?

Nearly arbitrary, like moonlight that actually belongs to the sun, the fasting month is only a cup holding light that is meant to spill over.

The moon, sacred symbol in Islam, is a heavenly body with no light of its own: Like a human it must reflect the animating light from without.

Yet the moon has its own characteristics—serenity, passion—and illustrates better than the sun our moods and wishes.

The moon draws the waters up the shores and sends them back down, and so beyond day or night the moon has real physical import, but quietly, mannered, internal.

The month moving backward through the year.

So a person could experience Ramadan in July when he is nine, again in July when he is around forty-five, and perhaps one more time when he is eighty.

Likewise, Ramadan in December when he is twenty-seven, again when he is sixty-two. He would like to see it a third time but he will have to live to nearly a hundred for that.

I have been much looking forward to Ramadan in winter, but suddenly now writing that I felt a very muffled and deeply covered river of fear. Instinctual of course, writing about my own mortality, getting older, being sixty, being eighty, wanting to be one hundred.

The month passes through the seasons, so too our own sense of youth and love passes through our physical lives many times, approaching then gone—approaching, then gone.

Reminding me how dangerous it was that I nearly lost myself, nearly gave myself over to living another person's life.

We are enjoined to eat well and celebrate once fasting is over yet here I am, dour son always, seeking to hold on to the fast, an earnest supplicant with passion to practice.

This weekend I took my nephew and niece to a contemporary art gallery. Jaffer, who is five, was entranced by an orange and red Rothko he called "the sunset." Alina's favorite was a darkened room with a blue-illuminated cavity gaping in the wall. The kids insisted we return once more to this space before leaving the gallery.

Their intellects are yet unspoiled and sharp with the fuel of pure emotional response; they understood these pieces. Though they had to be reminded by every guard we encountered not to touch the art.

This morning, reading a new translation of the Quran, I was shocked beyond understanding to read an alternate translation for the opening verse.

My entire life, I had had the deepest trouble with the verse "This is the Book. In it there is no doubt."

Which apparently can also be translated as "There is no doubt this book is a guide for the faithful."

Adrift now with the new line of Quran in my head. The book is meant to be thought about, reflected upon. As I have ever believed.

Adrift in the orange and blue of the art.

Adrift in the aftermath of the fast, eating again, feeling a little sick, unsure how to handle food, missing the physical sensation of hunger.

In other words a form of doubt but more accurately than doubt a desire to know.

A book is a guide. You wouldn't say "only a guide" because its influence is much bigger, bigger than the universe as a guide—a huge golden arrow pointing out into space, the way the golden arrows embedded on the ceilings of hotels in the Muslim world point in the direction of the *qibla*.

The rose is my qibla, wrote Sohrab Sepehri. *All the Heavens were a Bell—and Being but an Ear*, wrote Emily Dickinson.

The book and the fasting body both are guides. The body too can think. After all perhaps the mind is only the bard of the body, one of its constituent parts.

And the "self," the thing we call "I," floats across the surface of the mind like petals on a pond.

Each white fasting day trickles through the ghost-house of a month from darkness and absence to the full moon, and then wanes and wanes to the end.

Shape of the month's empty hallways, the shape of a fast in inverse. So each day is the opposite: one by one, one passes through.

And once the month is over you do what you do.

How do you hold it in your hand? The month grows full and then recedes. Re-seeds.

A month that is a petal floating in the cup of the year, which like a life lives in days, circular time, like a season or a year that goes in one direction but promises to return.

Recipes

Almond-Pear Oatmeal

INGREDIENTS

1 ripe Anjou pear

5 to 7 soft dates (any kind)

10-15 almonds

1 cup of rolled oats (not the quick cooking kind)

2 tablespoons of brown rice protein powder

1/4 cup of almond milk or soy milk

Little pinch of salt

PREPARATION

Cut the pear into small chunks.

Chop dates.

Break almonds into pieces with mortar and pestle.

INSTRUCTIONS

Cook rolled oats in boiling water.

As the oats become soft, add the dates and the brown rice powder and the salt.

As the liquid is absorbed, add the pears.

When the oatmeal becomes thick, add almond or soy milk to taste. Finish with the almonds. Alternately, the almonds can be added earlier and cooked with the oats. Serves two.

Aloo Chole

INGREDIENTS

2 cans of chickpeas

1 small can of tomato paste

1 medium onion

2 medium Yukon Golds or other firm yellow potato

2 tablespoons of Bibi's Masala Blend (see below)

2 tablespoons of coconut oil

2 tablespoons of strained Greek yogurt

PREPARATION

Dice the onion but not too finely. Medium (3/4 inch)
pieces are good.

Cut the potatoes into pieces not much bigger
than an inch.

Drain and rinse the chickpeas.

INSTRUCTIONS

Heat the coconut oil at medium heat in a medium
saucepot.

Add the onions. When translucent, add the yellow
potatoes.

Fry for a little while until the potatoes begin to soften;
add the chickpeas.

Add small bits of water to the masala blend to make a
liquidy paste. Add the masala paste and cook for a
little while before adding the tomato paste with a
little water if necessary.

Turn the heat to low and cover, cooking for 20-25 minutes. The longer you cook on lower heat, the more flavorful the curry will become.

Add additional salt or masala to taste. When cooked, turn off the heat and stir in the yogurt. Serve with brown rice.

Note: You can get a stronger, purer flavor by using dry chick peas. Soak overnight and rinse well before using. Skip the yogurt to go vegan.

Bibi's Masala Blend

Quantities listed below will yield several jars of masala mix. Because you will roast the spices before adding them to the mix, you can use the masala in cooking or to sprinkle on already cooked food. You can also use this masala in fruit salad or add to diced cucumbers and yogurt to make instant raita. This is the masala mix my mother makes, the taste of my childhood.

INGREDIENTS

2 cups of red chili powder
2 cup of coriander seeds
1/4 cup of cumin seeds
1/2 cup of garlic flakes or garlic powder
1/2 cup of salt (or to taste)
1/4 cup of mustard seeds (optional)
Pinches of fenugreek, to taste (optional)

PREPARATION

Excluding the red chili powder and the salt, roast each ingredient separately in a sauce pan. Using a food processor, pulverize the roasted seeds and garlic and then add the chili powder and salt, pulverizing all ingredients together until mixed well. Pour into jars. Jars will keep at room temperature for long periods but you can refrigerate larger portions for a year or more. Portions in this recipe can be adjusted proportionately to make larger or smaller batches.

Tanvir's Broccoli Salad

INGREDIENTS

3 cups chopped broccoli

1 cup Spanish peanuts (other kinds may become soggy)

1 cup golden raisins

2 chopped scallions (only the green portions)

1 cup mayonnaise or "nayonnaise" (vegan mayonnaise)

1 tablespoon granulated sugar

1 tablespoon white vinegar

Salt to taste

INSTRUCTIONS

Mix mayo or nayo, sugar and vinegar. Add together broccoli, peanuts, raisins and onions to a large bowl before tossing lightly with the dressing. Salt to taste.

Leftover Whole Grain Rice Pudding

Because whole grain rice does not keep as well as white rice, I often made rice pudding with any leftover rice; I've had best results with black rice and brown rice. This sweet treat can be enjoyed at the end of the day or in the morning for seher.

INGREDIENTS

Leftover rice

1 tablespoon of coconut oil.

Cardamom

Cloves

Cinnamon stick

One can of coconut milk

Salt to taste

Pure maple syrup

PREPARATION

Add water to the pot of leftover rice so rice is completely covered by a thin later of water. Break up any sticky chunks. Soak overnight.

INSTRUCTIONS

Turn the heat on low and add the coconut oil and the cinnamon stick. Cook the rice, stirring occasionally, adding small amounts of water to make it creamy. As the rice softens, add the salt and pinches of cardamom of clove to taste. Continue by adding coconut milk to desired consistency. Cook on low heat, stirring occasionally, for half an hour. Remove the cinnamon stick and sweeten to taste with maple syrup.

Alex's Chocolate Peanut Butter Vegan Ice Cream

INGREDIENTS

One cup raw cashews (unsalted)

Two cups soy milk

Four tablespoons cocoa powder

Half cup to one cup (according to taste) pure maple syrup

One creamy Hass avocado

Four tablespoons natural and unsalted peanut butter

One teaspoon salt

One tablespoon pure vanilla extract

PREPARATION

Soak cashews overnight.

INSTRUCTIONS

Drain cashews.

Add all ingredients to blender.

Blend until creamy.

Freeze.

Marco's Cardamom-Pistachio Vegan Ice Cream

In the previous recipe, substitute soaked raw (unroasted) pistachios for the peanut butter. In place of the cocoa powder substitute 2 level tablespoons powdered cardamom. You can add more powdered cardamom to taste. Remember that the mixture must taste stronger at room temperature to have good flavor in its frozen state.

Acknowledgments

The first part of this book originally appeared in an earlier version as a daily blog during August and September of 2009 on *Kenyon Review On-line* (www.kenyonreview.org/blog).

My thanks to Jim Schley for his interest in my work in general and his devoted attention to this book in particular—every word and line of it, every phrase.

My gratitude to Suzanne Strempek Shea and G. C. Waldrep, who gave me early encouragement. My thanks also to Jeffrey Levine, Josef Beery, and all at Tupelo Press for their hard work. Thank you to Caitlin Hamilton and Rick Summie and to JesseMiller for their support and assistance.

My endless appreciation and thanks to Marco Wilkinson, for infinities.

Finally, to Jaffery and Abid Sayeed, in whose house I had my first fasting experiences. Your kindness, generosity, laughter, and good spirits all live with me still. *In-al-ilahi-wa-In-al-alayhi-raji-oon.*

Other books from Tupelo Press:

See our complete backlist at www.tupelopress.org

Breinigsville, PA USA
03 April 2011
259027BV00001B/2/P